UNIVERSITY CASEBOOK SERIES®

2018 SUPPLEMENT TO

BUSINESS ORGANIZATIONS

CASES AND MATERIALS

UNABRIDGED AND CONCISE ELEVENTH EDITIONS

MELVIN ARON EISENBERG
The Jesse H. Choper Professor of Law, Emeritus
University of California at Berkeley

JAMES D. COX
Brainerd Currie Professor of Law
Duke University Law School

D1599536

FOUNDATION
PRESS

University Casebook Series is a trademark registered in the U.S. Patent and Trademark Office.

© 2017 LEG, Inc. d/b/a West Academic
© 2018 LEG, Inc. d/b/a West Academic
444 Cedar Street, Suite 700
St. Paul, MN 55101
1-877-888-1330

Printed in the United States of America

ISBN: 978-1-64242-028-9

ANALYTICAL TABLE OF CONTENTS

TABLE OF CASES

The principal cases are in bold type.

UNIVERSITY CASEBOOK SERIES®

2018 SUPPLEMENT TO

BUSINESS ORGANIZATIONS

CASES AND MATERIALS

**UNABRIDGED AND CONCISE
ELEVENTH EDITIONS**

CHAPTER 4

THE FOUNDATIONS OF A CORPORATION

7. THE SEDUCTIVE QUALITIES OF DEBT

Page 221. Add the following at the end of Note on the Tax Shield of Debt:

The tax shield provided by debt is no longer without limit. The multifaceted tax act passed in 2017 limits the amount a corporation is entitled to deduct as business interest in any taxable year beginning after December 31, 2017. The business interest deducted generally shall not exceed the sum of (i) the business interest income of the corporation for such taxable year plus (ii) 30% of the "adjusted taxable income" of the corporation for such taxable year. Until 2022, adjusted taxable income means the taxable income of the corporation before deduction of interest, depreciation or amortization (so-called "EBITA). In 2022, interests deductions become more constrained as adjustable taxable income when then mean taxable income (i.e., income after being reduced by any charges for interest, depreciation or amortization). The limitation does not apply to a corporation for a taxable year if the corporation's average annual gross receipts for the prior three taxable years does not exceed $25 million.

9. REQUISITES FOR VALID ACTION BY THE BOARD

Page 229.[1] Insert the following after *Fogel v. U.S. Energy Systems, Inc.*:

NOTE ON DISGRUNTLED DIRECTORS PLOTTING TO FIRE THE CEO

Klaassen v. Allegro Dev. Corp., 106 A.3d 1035 (Del. 2014), reached a different result than *Fogel*. Allegro Development Corporation had a board of five directors, one of which was Klaassen; in several phone calls the four outside directors discussed their rising unhappiness with Klaassen and plotted to terminate him at the upcoming regularly scheduled November board meeting. In preparation for this meeting, Hood, one of the outside directors, spoke with Klaassen to make sure that he would have Allegro's general counsel in attendance at the November meeting as the board may need legal guidance should it decide to exercise its redemption option on some outstanding shares. This was a false statement as the real reason for the outside directors wanting counsel to be there was to handle details of Klaassen's termination. At the November board meeting, the four outside directors fired Klaassen and appointed Hood to be the new CEO. Klaassen initially was cooperative; he worked with Hood and others on the transition

---

in the executive suite and negotiated an agreement for him to be an "Executive Consultant" to Allegro. Time, however, did not heal all wounds. Seven months after being fired, Klaassen sued, alleging that his termination was invalid because he did not receive any pre-meeting notice that his termination would be considered and that he had been deceived as to the purpose of the meeting by Hood's failure to state the real purpose of wishing counsel to attend the November meeting was to handle legal issues related to his termination. The Delaware Supreme Court held that because Klaassen's termination occurred at a regular board meeting no advance notice of the matter was required. With respect to Klaassen's claim he had been deceived, the court concluded the claim was equitable in nature and, contrary to language in *Fogel*, deception gives rise to a voidable, not a void, claim. The Supreme Court affirmed the Court of Chancery's holding that Klaassen's claim was barred because Klaassen's cooperation following his termination established the equitable defense of acquiescence.

10. THE NORMAL REQUISITES FOR VALID SHAREHOLDER ACTION

Page 234.[2] Insert the following at the end of the section:

Gwyn R. Hartman Revocable Living Trust v. S. Mich. Bancorp, Inc.

United States Court of Appeals for the Sixth Circuit, 2015.
780 F.3d 724.

■ SUTTON, CIRCUIT JUDGE.

Whenever a Michigan corporation holds a shareholder meeting, it must disclose any proposals on the agenda that a shareholder wishes to submit for shareholder action. . . .

Bancorp's bylaws do not permit the corporation to claw back fees paid to directors found liable for breaching their fiduciary duties. In 2012, the Gwyn R. Hartman Revocable Living Trust, a Bancorp shareholder, drafted a one-paragraph resolution exhorting Bancorp's board to fill that gap. It asked the board to include the resolution in Bancorp's proxy statement for the upcoming annual meeting along with a two-paragraph "supporting statement" invoking the need for more "director accountability." . . .

The board refused. Its March 2013 proxy statement told shareholders merely that a shareholder planned to propose a resolution urging the board to amend the company's bylaws. If that resolution materialized, the statement continued, the directors would use their "discretionary authority" to vote it down by treating all submitted proxies as no-votes absent instructions to the contrary. R. 24 at 2. The statement said nothing else about the proposal or its substance.

---

[2] Page 152 in Concise edition.

When the annual meeting convened a month or so later, the trust's representative objected to the sufficiency of the disclosure, and objected again when the proposal came up for a vote. The vote did not go the trust's way. Just 150,000 shares favored the proposal, and more than 1.7 million shares opposed it.

The trust sued Bancorp and John H. Castle, the company's chairman and CEO, for "intentional[ly] withholding" its proposal from the proxy statement and for "denying" the trust "any meaningful opportunity to solicit votes." . . . The district court dismissed the complaint for failing to state a claim on which relief could be granted.

. . .

The relevant Michigan statute requires companies to give shareholders "written notice of the time, place if any, and purposes" of any upcoming meeting. Mich. Comp. Laws § 450.1404. "[N]otice of the purposes of a meeting," the statute continues, "shall include notice of shareholder proposals" that a shareholder intends to submit for a vote. *Id.* We are hard-pressed to understand how mere acknowledgement of the existence of a proposal—without describing even its subject matter— amounts to "notice" under the statute. . . .

[T]he Michigan courts have not looked kindly on bare-bones disclosures of this ilk. In *Bourne v. Sanford*, 327 Mich. 175, 41 N.W.2d 515 (Mich. 1950), the directors tried to convene a board meeting to dissolve a company without letting its only shareholder know. That was impermissible, the Court held: "We can hardly conceive of an occasion when it is more vital to have a meeting at which there could be a general discussion, interchange of views and consultation of the directors." *Id.* at 521–22. Had the shareholder been properly notified, he could have prepared for the meeting, made his case, and perhaps changed the outcome. *Id.* at 522. A state appellate court . . . concluded that Michigan's "purpose-notice" requirement is designed to help shareholders "study [a] proposal, arrive at a position, and either oppose it or support it" before the meeting itself. *Id.* at 546.

Bancorp's notice did not satisfy these requirements. Its proxy statement said merely that a shareholder intended to submit a resolution calling upon the board to amend the company's bylaws. But it never specified *which* bylaw or *what* topic the bylaw covered. With such skeletal "disclosure" in hand, a shareholder would never know whether the resolution sought to change the bylaws' record-date procedure or their compensation-committee guidelines or their indemnification rules or their amendment restrictions or their discussion of director liability. *Cf. Horbal v. St. John's Greek Catholic Church of Detroit*, 260 Mich. 331, 244 N.W. 493, 495 (Mich. 1932) (holding that an ecclesiastical corporation violated an analogous requirement by mortgaging its property at a special meeting that its notice described only as involving a "very important" matter, full stop).

Other States have endorsed the principles set forth in *Bourne* and *Darvin.* . . . Delaware's General Corporation Law requires a company to give shareholders a summary of only a few types of proposed action. *See* Del. Code Ann. tit. 8, § 242(b)(1). Its courts, however, have plugged the gaps in that regime with a broader duty of disclosure. *See Stroud v. Grace*, 606 A.2d 75, 85–88 (Del. 1992). These endorsements make clear that, at a minimum, a meeting notice "should sufficiently apprise [shareholders] of matters to be considered at the meeting, give them information upon which they may exercise intelligent judgment with reference to the proposed questions, and open up avenues for obtaining additional information." 5 Fletcher Cyclopedia of the Law of Corporations § 2008 (2014). . . .

For these reasons, we reverse the district court's judgment and remand for further proceedings.

11. THE ELECTION OF DIRECTORS

A. STAGGERED BOARDS

Page 235.[3] **Substitute the following for the Kahan & Rock excerpt:**

A staggered board, particularly in conjunction with the ubiquitous poison pill, is a potent and controversial defense against a corporate takeover. As illustrated earlier, replacing a majority of a board of directors on a staggered board takes two consecutive annual shareholders meetings. Commentators and activists have argued that the staggered board and poison pill combination entrenches managers and should be disallowed by courts. Indeed, a staggered board "is the most powerful takeover defense available." Michael Klausner, The Empirical Revolution in Law: Fact and Fiction in Corporate Law and Governance, 65 Stan. L. Rev. 1325, 1352–53 (2013).

Because altering the procedures for electing directors requires an amendment to the article of incorporation, the status quo was thought to be that boards of companies without staggered boards wanted to adopt them, but could not without shareholder approval, while shareholders of companies with staggered boards wanted to eliminate them, but could not without board approval. Illustrating this situation, 44% of S&P 100 Companies had a staggered board in 2003. This paradigm has ended as more and more corporations, particularly the largest ones, declassify (de-stagger) their boards. Indeed, the move to a declassified board has happened quickly among large companies. Thus, in 2009 only 16% of S&P 100 Companies had a staggered board, whereas in 2003 44% of them had staggered boards. Marcel Kahan & Edward Rock, Embattled CEOS, 88 Tex. L. Rev. 987, 1007–09 (2010). As the table below reflects, among the largest companies a classified board is the exception and not the rule.

---

[3]   Page 153 in the Concise edition.

Board elections	S&P 500	S&P MidCap 400	S&P SmallCap 600	S&P 1500	Russell 3000
Annual elections	90%	64%	55%	69%	59%
Majority voting in director elections	89%	62%	43%	64%	47%

Ernst & Young Global Limited, EY Center for Board Matters: Corporate Governance By The Numbers, Board Elections, (Mark Manoff & Stephen W. Klemash, eds., 2017) (current as of Mar. 31 2017) *available at* http://www.ey.com/us/en/issues/governance-and-reporting/ey-corporate-governance-by-the-numbers#boardelections.

As the table shows, 90% of S&P 500 Companies now hold annual elections for the full board of directors. While staggered boards remain more prevalent among smaller firms, they have followed the largest companies' lead and begun de-staggering. Incidence of staggered boards in S&P MidCap 400 companies decreased from 67% in 2003 to 36% in 2017. Among S&P SmallCap 600 companies incidence decreased from 61% in 2003 to 45% in 2017. What explains why classified boards become more common as firm size declines?

Whether this shift creates value for shareholders is the subject of an ongoing debate. *Compare* Lucian Arye Bebchuk, John C. Coates & Guhan Subramanian, The Powerful Antitakeover Force of Staggered Boards: Theory, Evidence, and Policy, 54 Stan. L. Rev. 887, 926–27 (2002) (finding empirical evidence that staggered boards have a negative impact on firm value); Lucian A. Bebchuk & Alma Cohen, The Costs of Entrenched Boards, 78 J. Fin. Econ. 409, 410 (2005) (associating staggered boards with lower firm value). Alma Cohen & Charles C.Y. Wang, How Do Staggered Boards Affect Shareholder Value? Evidence from a Natural Experiment, 110 J. Fin. Econ. 627 (2013) (finding that staggered board *cause* a firm to have a lower value) *with* K.J. Martin Cremers and Simone M. Sepe, The Shareholder Value of Empowered Boards, 68 Stan. L. Rev. 67 (2016) (showing evidence that measures that empower directors, such as staggered boards, enhance firm value).

C. PLURALITY VOTING

Page 241.[4] Substitute the following for the Kahan & Rock excerpt:

Between 2003 and 2009, majority voting went from the outlier within the S&P 100 (10%) to the dominant majority (90%). The rapid adoption of majority voting led "experienced observers like Martin Lipton [to opine] that '. . . majority voting will become universal.'" Marcel Kahan & Edward Rock, Embattled CEOS, 88 Tex. L. Rev. 987, 1010–11 (2010). Though majority voting has not been adopted as widely by smaller companies, there has been a substantial increase in the rate of majority

---

[4]   Page 155 in the Concise edition.

voting in companies outside of the S&P 500 as well. *Id.* In 2009, only 17% of companies outside the S&P 500 had adopted majority voting. *Id.* As the table shows, 62% of S&P MidCap 400 companies, 43% of S&P SmallCap 600 companies, and 43% of Russell 3000 companies now use majority voting in director elections.

Though majority voting has become the new standard, it has had very little effect on the election of directors. A recent study reported that only eight of more than twenty-four thousand nominees at S&P 1500 companies that used majority voting between 2007 and 2013 did not receive a majority of votes, and only three of those ultimately lost their seat. Stephen J. Choi et al., Does Majority Voting Improve Board Accountability?, 83 U. Chi. L. Rev. 1119, 1122 (2016). This apparent impotence led Professors Jie Cai, Jacqueline Garner, and Ralph Walkling to label majority voting a "paper tiger." Jay Cai et al., A Paper Tiger? An Empirical Analysis of Majority Voting, 21 J. Corp. Fin. 119, 133 (2013). Others argue that though majority voting has had almost no direct impact on elections, it has had a number of indirect effects such as a positive abnormal increase in stock price, a higher rate of shareholder-proposal implementation, and a lower rate of consecutive elections with a large number of votes withheld. Yonca Ertimur, et al., Does the Director Election System Matter? Evidence from Majority Voting, 20 Rev. Accounting Stud. 1, 6–32 (2015). Interestingly, empirical evidence suggests that majority voting may have a greater impact on firms that adopt it later (i.e., late adopters) relative to their peers (early adopters). In other words, early adopters already had shareholder-friendly governance and were less in need of implementing majority voting. On the other hand, majority voting has made late adopters more shareholder-friendly. Stephen J. Choi et al., Does Majority Voting Improve Board Accountability?, 83 U. Chi. L. Rev. 1119, 1123–24 (2016).

12. REMOVAL OF DIRECTORS

Page 243.[5] Insert the following before Note on the Removal of Directors:

In re VAALCO Energy Shareholder Litig.
Delaware Chancery Court, 2015.
CA No. 11775–VCL.
Transcript 62–66.

[For many years, VAALCO Energy, Inc. had a classified board so that its directors served three-year terms with only one-third of the board elected annually. Both its charter and bylaws provided that the directors could only be removed for cause. In 2009, VAALCO declassified its board, but did not change its charter provision that continued to provide that shareholders could only remove a director for cause. Following a near 80

---

[5]   Page 156 in Concise edition.

percent decline in its stock price in 2014, relations between its management and shareholders deteriorated. A shareholder group ("the Group 42") owning about 11 percent of the company filed Schedule 13D announcing they could seek changes in VAALCO's board and senior management. The filing prompted management to adopt a poison pill and several other defensive measures. Thereafter Group 42 announced it would seek to remove and replace the VAALCO directors at a special stockholders' meeting. The announcement explained that Group 42 believed directors could be removed under Delaware Section 141(k) with or without cause, since the board was neither classified nor elected via cumulative voting. VAALCO asserted its charter was controlling so that removal could only occur for cause. Litigation ensued. Days before the special shareholder meeting, Vice-Chancellor Lassiter, ruling from the bench, granted Group 42's motion for summary judgment on the issue:]

I do believe that [VAALCO's] Article V, Section 3 of the charter and Article III, Section 2 of the bylaws, which provide for only for-cause removal in the context of a nonclassified board, conflict with Section 141(k) of the Delaware General Corporation Law and are, therefore, invalid. This analysis is driven by the plain language of 141(k). 141(k) states affirmatively "Any director or the entire board of directors may be removed, with or without cause, by the holders of a majority of the shares then entitled to vote at an election of directors . . . ." That is the rule. It then continues. So technically it's a comma and identifies two exceptions: "except as follows:" One exception is " . . . a corporation whose board is classified as provided in subsection (d) . . . ." Another exception is subsection 2, "In the case of a board of directors having cumulative voting . . . ." For better or for worse, those are the two statutory exceptions. . . .

What I think is the defendants' strongest argument against the plain language of 141(k) and this reading is the language in 141(d), which, for better or for worse, says that "The directors of any corporation organized under this chapter may, by the certificate of incorporation or by an initial bylaw, or by a bylaw adopted by a vote of the stockholder, be divided into 1, 2 or 3 classes . . . ." This creates, at least on its face, the somewhat oxymoronic concept of a single-class classified board. As the defendants see that, that single-class board would be classified and, hence, the directors only would be subject to removal for cause. That, I think, is a pretty novel reading of 141(d). I don't think anybody out there has ever touted the idea of single-class classified boards triggering removal for cause. . . .

Here, what we have is a declassified straight board. We have a declassified straight board that does not try to get into 141(k)(1) that way but, rather, admits that it is a straight board. . . .

CHAPTER 5

THE LEGAL STRUCTURE OF PUBLICLY HELD CORPORATIONS

2. CORPORATE GOVERNANCE AND THE RISE OF INSTITUTIONAL SHAREHOLDERS

A. SHAREHOLDER VOTING

Page 296.[1] Insert the following after paragraph discussing _Providence & Worcester Co. v. Baker_:

Delaware upheld a plan to establish "tenure voting" in _Williams v. Geier_, 671 A.2d 1368 (Del. 1996), whereby the company's shareholders approved a recapitalization in which each share would initially have ten votes; however, upon a change in ownership, a share would revert to having one vote until it was held for three years (shares held in street name were presumed to have short-term owners and relegated to one vote per share).

Because there is evidence that the holding period of institutional investors is measured in weeks, and not months, there is growing concern whether institutions seek only short-term gains so that their short-termism inhibits company managers from pursuing long-terms strategies that are better for the firm. _See_ David J. Berger, Steven Davidoff Solomon & Aaron J. Benjamin, Tenure Voting and the U.S. Public Company, 72 Bus. Law. 295 (2017); Lynne L. Dallas & Jordan M. Barry, Long-Term Shareholders and Time-Phased Voting, 40 Del. J. Corp. L. 541 (2016)(a 1980 investment in 12 companies that maintained tenure voting through 2013 yielded return six time greater than the S&P 500). To those who believe short-termism is harmful, devices like tenure voting are one of the antidotes.

Another approach is dual-class shares whereby the class of common shares issued insiders have super-voting rights whereas shares issued to the public carry one vote per share. It is not unusual in IPOs firms to have such a dual class structure. Indeed, when Snap, Inc. (a/k/a Snap Chat) went public only non-voting common shares were sold the public; a handful of its managers held all the voting shares. Earlier, the SEC's attempted to prohibit the exchanges from listing dual-class shares, but the court held the SEC lacked authority to enter this area. Business Roundtable v. SEC, 905 F.2d 406 (D.C. Cir. 1990). Nonetheless, the exchanges were pressured by the SEC with the end result they adopted voting rights policies that restrict dual-class and tenure voting structures unless they are in place when the company

---

[1]   Page 204 in Concise edition.

went public, such as what occurred with Snap, Inc. *See* NYSE Rule 313.00(A); Nasdaq Rule 5640.

Super voting shares, particularly those issued initially to the firm's founders, raise concerns whether, at least over time, the arrangement exacerbates agency costs by the twin effects of insider have voting power being disproportionate to their equity in the firm and that the super voting power entrenches existing management. *See e.g.,* Ronald Masulis, Cong Wang & Fei Xie, Agency Problems at Dual-Class Companies, 64 J. Fin. 1697 (2009)(finding that the greater that the insider's percentage of total voting power exceeds equity ownership the greater the evidence of high compensation, value destroying acquisitions, and lower returns on capital investment decisions). Lucian A. Bebchuk & Kobi Kastiel, The Untenable Case for Perpetual Dual-Class Stock, 103 Va. L. Rev. 585, 590 (2017)("as time passes, the potential costs of a dual-class structure tend to increase while the potential benefits tend to erode" so that debate should focus on barring such voting structures or mandating they end after a fixed period of time).

B. FINANCIAL INSTITUTIONS AND THEIR ADVISORS

Page 314.[2] Insert the following at the beginning of the note following the principal insert:

Further investigation of the effects of hedge funds activism in 2008–14 finds that activist funds producing the most positive results achieve success not solely by the targets they select but because of their reputation that has been earned through prior successful engagements. This cohort of top performing hedge funds engage in fewer campaigns, but target much larger and more profitable firms than the poorer performing hedge funds.

> The Top Investor Hedge Funds . . . had greater financial clout; they had existed for longer than other activists and had significantly larger assets under management. They also had greater expertise; they had a greater ability to force board changes at the firms they target. Top Investor Hedge Funds specifically stated an intent to replace directors, were more involved in proxy fights and lawsuits, and won three times as many proxy fights and lawsuits as other activists. They also target more entrenched firms indicating higher agency costs, but, nevertheless, were more successful in gaining board seats, and implementing changes after intervening, improving operating performance.

C.N.V. Krishnan, Frank Partnoy & Randall S. Thomas, The Second Wave of Hedge Fund Activism: The Importance of Reputation, Clout, and Expertise, J. Corp. Fin. 296, 314 (2016).

---

[2]   Page 219 in the Concise edition.

CHAPTER 6

SHAREHOLDER INFORMATIONAL RIGHTS & PROXY VOTING

1. SHAREHOLDER INFORMATION RIGHTS UNDER STATE AND FEDERAL LAW

E. PERIODIC DISCLOSURE UNDER THE SECURITIES EXCHANGE ACT

Page 355.[1] Add the following after Note in Periodic Reporting by Registered Corporations:

NOTE ON VANISHING HOLDERS AND LISTED COMPANIES

The number of record holders of public companies is declining, if not in freefall. About one-fifth of the largest 1500 companies have fewer than 300 record holders. "Among all stocks tracked by S&P Dow Jones Indices, shareholders of record have shrunk to a median of 352 today from 1,626 two decades ago." Zweig, Disappearing From View: America's Shareholders, Wall St. J. at B–7 (June 11, 2016).

Record holders are not the only disappearing act. In an important study, Professors Doidge, Karolyi and Stulz find that at least in the U.S. public listings have seriously declined so that they are 39 percent lower than they were 20 years ago. Since robust capital markets are widely believed to signal economic vitality, is the decline in listings to be seen as the canary in the mine? Can the decline in listings over the past 20 years relative to the experience in other markets be attributed to over regulation?

> The U.S. has experienced a dramatic decrease in the number of publicly-listed firms whereas listings increased in the rest of the world. As a result, the U.S. has developed a listing gap compared to other countries and this gap has become large, exceeding 5,000 firms. . . . The listing gap does not arise because there are fewer firms or startups. Though the size of the smallest listed firms is larger at the end of our sample than at the listing peak, all listed firms have generally become larger. While these changes indicate that the exchanges have become less hospitable to the smallest firms, the probability that a firm is listed has fallen for all firm sizes, albeit less so for the very largest firms. We conclude that firm size alone cannot explain the listing gap.

---

[1] Page 256 in Concise edition.

Before the listing peak in 1996, the net new list rate in the U.S. was positive. After 1996, it was negative because the delist rate increased and the new list rate fell. We show that if the new list and delist rates from the pre-peak period applied after 1996, there would be no gap today. Similarly, the net new list rate in non-U.S. countries was positive and sufficiently large after 1996 that there would be no gap if the U.S. had had new list and delist rates similar to these countries.

The listing gap cannot be explained by just the decrease in the new list rate. We show that the U.S. would still have a listing gap if the new list rate had not fallen. To explain the gap, one has to explain *both* the fall in the new list rate *and* the rise in the delist rate. We show that the delist rate rose because of an increase in merger activity involving publicly-listed targets. After 1996, the percentage of firms delisted for cause did not increase, but the percentage of firms delisted because of a merger did. Much has been made of the increase in firms going dark or going private after SOX. We show that the percentage of firms delisting voluntarily is too small to explain the listing gap or even to contribute meaningfully to closing the gap.

Doidge, *et al.*, The U.S. Listing Gap, NBER Working Paper No. 21181 (May 2015). Note the authors reflect that the percentage of "startup" firms going public has steadily declined over the years and that the percentage of startups going public has similarly declined.

2. THE PROXY RULES: AN INTRODUCTION

Page 357.[2] Add the following to the end of the carryover paragraph at the top of the page:

The "Universal Proxy." In 2017, the SEC proposed the use of a "universal proxy" as a means to accommodate activist shareholders who advance a short slate of nominees. Absent a universal proxy only shareholders who attend the meeting can as a practical matter vote for nominees on both management and the dissident proxies. As a practical matter, a shareholder who does not attend the stockholder meeting is unable to vote for some management's nominees and vote for the nominees of the dissidents on the dissident's proxy. This is because under corporate law, if a shareholder submits two different proxies, the most recently executed proxy is counted on the theory that it revokes the proxy of the earlier exercised proxy. The dissident can try to overcome this feature by including on its proxy not only its nominees but also some of management's nominees so that solicited shareholders have a sense they are voting for the exact number of nominees as there are seats up for election. But the management nominees the dissident chooses to include may well not be the nominees the shareholder would have preferred among the larger set of management nominees. The universal proxy overcomes this problem. As proposed by the

---

[2]   Page 258 of the Concise edition.

SEC, when there is a contested board election, the proxy used by management and the insurgent must include the names of all the nominees, those of management and those of the insurgent, so that shareholders can thereby choose among all the candidates rather than being forced into an all-or-nothing choice. Contestants, however, will have to direct shareholders to each other's proxy statements for information regarding the background of their respective candidates.

Page 358.[3] Add the following at the end of Note 3:

Despite the anti-bundling rule and court decisions enforcing the rule, bundling continues to vex investors. *See* James D. Cox, Fabrizio Ferri, Colleen Honigsberg & Randall S. Thomas, Quieting the Shareholders' Voice: Empirical Evidence of Pervasive Bundling in Proxy Solicitations, 89 S. Cal. L. Rev 1175 (2016)(study of 1300 management proposal for amendments to articles or bylaws finding 28.8 percent were coupled with unrelated matters with 6.2 percent coupling a material negative value proposal with a material positive value proposal).

Page 361.[4] Add the following to the bottom of the page:

Rule 14a–2(b)(1) exempts from the filing and delivery requirements a communication by any person "who does not, at any time during such solicitation, seek directly or indirectly, . . . the power to act as proxy for a security holder and does not furnish or otherwise request" a form of proxy. The breadth of this provision has always been a matter of some doubt. In adopting the provision, the SEC observed it feared that without this exemption "every expression of opinion concerning a publicly-traded corporation . . . would [due to the breadth of "proxy" and "solicitation" as defined in its rules] raise serious questions under the [F]ree [S]peech [C]lause of the First Amendment."

Rule 14a–2(b)(1) clearly reaches recommendations that proxy advisors provide their clients. But, as illustrated by *Gas Natural, Inc. v. Osborne*, 2015 U.S. App. LEXIS 15277 (Sixth Cir. Aug. 27, 2015), it is a good deal broader than that. Osborne had been terminated as Gas Natural's CEO, and removed from its slate of nominees for the upcoming annual board election. Three weeks before the stockholder meeting, Osborne wrote to the shareholders criticizing Gas Natural's management and "ask[ed] for [the shareholders'] help in running these greedy individuals out of our company." In subsequent communications he referred to the directors and officers as Nazis, claimed the company was broke, and criticized the decision to rehire its former chief operating officer. Contemporaneous with his initial letter, he requested a list of the stockholders as well as the NOBO list, stating he wished the lists "so I can solicit their support to be reinstated to the Board." He later testified he wanted "to put forward a slate of [directors] who would be supportive of his views." However, he never put forth such a slate and did not directly or indirectly seek the power to act as proxy for another shareholder. The district court, on the strength of *Okin*, granted a permanent

---

[3]   Page 259 in Concise edition.

[4]   Page 263 after the second paragraph in Concise edition.

injunction against Osborne for not complying with the filing and delivery requirements of the proxy rules. The Sixth Circuit reversed, finding the communication fell within Rule 14a–(2)(b)(1); the panel believed a fair reading of the communications did request "shareholders to withhold or revoke proxies for the" upcoming meeting, Osborne did not request authority to act as a proxy. As such, the communications fell squarely within the scope of the exemption which excludes communications that does not request the shareholders to execute proxies, does not request authority to act as proxy for any shareholder, and that does not include a proxy form. Furthermore, the Sixth Circuit found that none of the enumerated exceptions to the exemption applied.

3.   THE PROXY RULES: SHAREHOLDER ACCESS

B.   SHAREHOLDER PROPOSALS UNDER RULE 14a–8

Page 370.[5] Insert the following case at the top of the page before the excerpt by Thomas & Cotter:

Trinity Wall St. v. Wal-Mart Stores, Inc.

United States Court of Appeals for the Third Circuit, 2015.
792 F.3d 323.

■ AMBRO, CIRCUIT JUDGE.

I.   INTRODUCTION

"[T]he secret of successful retailing is to give your customers what they want." Sam Walton, Sam Walton: Made in America 173 (1993). This case involves one shareholder's attempt to affect how Wal-Mart goes about doing that.

Appellant Wal-Mart Stores, Inc., the world's largest retailer, and one of its shareholders, Appellee Trinity Wall Street—an Episcopal parish headquartered in New York City that owns Wal-Mart stock—are locked in a heated dispute. It stems from Wal-Mart's rejection of Trinity's request to include its shareholder proposal in Wal-Mart's proxy materials for shareholder consideration.

. . .

Wal-Mart obtained what is known as a "no-action letter" from the staff of the SEC's Division of Corporate Finance (the "Corp. Fin. staff" or "staff"), thus signaling that there would be no recommendation of an enforcement action against the company if it omitted the proposal from its proxy materials. . . . Trinity thereafter filed suit in federal court, seeking to enjoin Wal-Mart's exclusion of the proposal. . . . [T]he District Court . . . [held] that, because the proposal concerned the company's Board (rather than its management) and focused principally on

---

[5]   Page 265 Concise edition.

governance (rather than how Wal-Mart decides what to sell), it was outside Wal-Mart's ordinary business operations. Wal-Mart appeals. . . .

Stripped to its essence, Trinity's proposal—although styled as promoting improved governance—goes to the heart of Wal-Mart's business: what it sells on its shelves. For the reasons that follow, we hold that it is excludable under Rule 14a–8(i)(7) and reverse the ruling of the District Court.

II. FACTS & PROCEDURAL HISTORY

. . .

A. Trinity Objects to Wal-Mart's Sale of Assault Rifles.

Trinity's roots extend back centuries. Its St. Paul's Chapel is the oldest public building in continuous use in New York City and is where George Washington worshipped after his first inauguration. In 1705, the church was the beneficiary of the lower Manhattan farm of Queen Anne of England, instantly making it very wealthy.

The story isn't much different today. Trinity continues to be one of the wealthiest religious institutions in the United States, with a balance sheet of over $800 million in assets and real estate valued at approximately $3 billion. . . . Its strong financial footing, according to Trinity, empowers it to "pursue a mission of good works beyond the reach of other religious institutions." . . . Part of that mission is to reduce violence in society.

Alarmed by the spate of mass murders in America, in particular the shooting at Sandy Hook Elementary School in December 2012, Trinity resolved to use its investment portfolio to address the ease of access to rifles equipped with high-capacity magazines (the weapon of choice of the Sandy Hook shooter and other mass murderers). Its principal focus was Wal-Mart.

During its review of Wal-Mart's merchandising practices, Trinity discovered what it perceived as a major inconsistency. Despite the retailer's stated mission to "make a difference on the big issues that matter to us all," . . . it continued in some states to sell the Bushmaster AR-15 (a model of assault rifle). Trinity also perceived Wal-Mart as taking an unprincipled approach in deciding which products to sell. For example, despite its position on the AR-15, Wal-Mart does not sell adult-rated movie titles (i.e., those rated NC-17) or similarly rated video or computer games. Nor does it sell to children under 17 " 'R' rated movies or 'Mature' rated video games." . . . also doesn't sell "music bearing a 'Parental Advisory Label' " because of concerns about the music containing "strong language or depictions of violence, sex, or substance abuse." *Id.* And apparently due to safety concerns, it has stopped selling (1) handguns in the United States; (2) high-capacity magazines separate from a gun; and (3) guns through its website. . . . Trinity attributes these perceived inconsistencies to the "lack of written policies and Board oversight concerning its approach to products that could have momentous consequences for both society and corporate reputation and brand value[.]" . . .

B. Trinity's Shareholder Proposal. . . .

Trinity drafted a shareholder proposal aimed at filling the governance gap it perceived. The proposal, which is the subject of this appeal, provides:

Resolved:

Stockholders request that the Board amend the Compensation, Nominating and Governance Committee charter . . . as follows:

"27. Providing oversight concerning [and the public reporting of] the formulation and implementation of . . . policies and standards that determine whether or not the Company should sell a product that:

1) especially endangers public safety and well-being;

2) has the substantial potential to impair the reputation of the Company; and/or

3) would reasonably be considered by many offensive to the family and community values integral to the Company's promotion of its brand."

. . .

The proposal also included a supporting statement asserting in relevant part that

[t]he company respects family and community interests by choosing not to sell certain products such as music that depicts violence or sex and high capacity magazines separately from a gun, but lacks policies and standards to ensure transparent and consistent merchandizing decisions across product categories. This results in the company's sale of products, such as guns equipped with high capacity magazines, that facilitate mass killings, even as it prohibits sales of passive products such as music that merely depict such violent rampages.

. . . .

While guns equipped with high capacity magazines are just one example of a product whose sale poses significant risks to the public and to the company's reputation and brand, their sale illustrates a lack of reasonable consistency that this proposal seeks to address through Board level oversight. . . .

III. REGULATORY BACKGROUND

. . .

D. Exclusion of Shareholder Proposals

Though the Rule 14a–8 option is financially advantageous, it does not "create an open forum for shareholder communication." . . . Rule 14a–

8 restricts the company-subsidy to "shareholders who offer 'proper' proposals." . . . A "proper" proposal is one that doesn't fit within one of Rule 14a–8's exclusionary grounds—which are both substantive and procedural.

. . .

E. SEC Interpretive Releases on the "Ordinary Business" Exclusion

The ordinary business exclusion has been called the "most perplexing" of all the 14a–8 bars. See Daniel E. Lazaroff, *Promoting Corporate Democracy and Social Responsibility: The Need to Reform the Federal Proxy Rules on Shareholder Proposals*, 50 Rutgers L. Rev. 33, 94 (1997). This stems from the opaque term "ordinary business," which is neither self-defining nor consistent in its meaning across different corporate contexts. . . .

3.   The 1982 Proposing Release

. . . In 1982 . . . the staff's then-prevailing view on proposals that ask a company to (1) prepare a report to shareholders or (2) recommend that a special committee be formed to examine a particular area of its business. . . . [was they] were not excludable even if the subject matter of the report or examination involved an ordinary business matter because, in its view, a company doesn't disseminate reports to shareholders or establish special committees as part of its ordinary business operations. *See id.*

. . .

4.   The 1983 Adopting Release

After notice and comment, the Commission . . . [concluded that] [b]ecause [the staff's] interpretation raises form over substance and renders the provisions of [the ordinary business exclusion] largely a nullity. . . . It thus directed the staff to "consider whether the subject matter of a special report or the committee involves a matter of ordinary business; where it does, the proposal will be excludable." *Id.*

5.   The 1997 Proposing Release

The SEC revisited the ordinary business exclusion in the late 1990s to tackle proposals "relating simultaneously to both an 'ordinary business' matter and a significant social policy issue." . . . The interpretive snag was that the "fairly straightforward mission" of the rule was ill-suited to address contemporary social issues and "provided no guidance" on how to treat proposals raising such issues. *Id.* This difficulty showed itself when the staff allowed a company (Cracker Barrel Old Country Stores) to exclude a proposal that asked it to "prohibit discrimination on the basis of sexual orientation." *New York City Emps.' Ret. Sys. v. S.E.C.*, 45 F.3d 7, 9 (2d Cir. 1995). In handling the proposal, the staff espoused the view . . . that employment-related proposals— regardless whether they raise a social issue—are categorically excludable. *See Cracker Barrel Old Country Store, Inc.*, SEC No-Action Letter, 1992 SEC No-Act. LEXIS 984, 1992 WL 289095, at *1 (Oct. 13, 1992) ("[T]he Division has determined that the fact that a shareholder proposal concerning a company's employment policies and practices for the general workforce is tied to a social issue will no longer be viewed as removing the proposal from the realm of ordinary business operations of the registrant. Rather, determinations with respect to any such proposals are governed by the employment-based nature of the proposal."). To end this practice, the SEC . . . [proposed] that "employment-related proposals focusing on significant social policy issues could not automatically be excluded under the 'ordinary business' exclusion." 1997 Proposing Release, 1997 SEC LEXIS 1962, 1997 WL 578696, at *13. And going forward, "the 'bright line' approach for employment-related proposals established by the Cracker Barrel position would be replaced by a case-by-case analysis that prevailed previously." *Id.*

. . .

6.   The 1998 Adopting Release

Yet again the SEC declined to modify the language of the rule, perhaps afraid to unleash unintended consequences. . . . It elected simply to reverse the Staff's 1992 *Cracker Barrel* no-action letter, thus "return[ing] to the case-by-case analytical approach. . . . It also reaffirmed that the term "ordinary business" continues to 'refer[ ] to matters *that are not necessarily 'ordinary' in the common meaning of the word"* and 'is rooted in the corporate law concept providing management with flexibility in directing certain core matters involving the company's business and operations.' " . . .

With that background, we move to the merits of Wal-Mart's appeal.

IV. ANALYSIS

. . .

A.   Trinity's Proposal Relates to Wal-Mart's Ordinary Business Operations.

We employ a two-part analysis to determine whether Trinity's proposal "deals with a matter relating to the company's ordinary business operations[.]" 17 C.F.R. § 240.14a–8(i)(7). Under the first step, we discern the "subject matter" of the proposal. *See* 1983 Adopting Release, 1983 SEC LEXIS 1011, 1983 WL 33272, at *7. Under the second, we ask whether that subject matter relates to Wal-Mart's ordinary business operations. *Id.* If the answer to the second question is yes, Wal-Mart must still convince us that Trinity's proposal does not raise a significant policy issue that transcends the nuts and bolts of the retailer's business.

1. What is the subject matter of Trinity's proposal?

. . .

Trinity argues that the subject matter of its proposal is the improvement of "corporate governance over strategic matters of community responsibility, reputation for good corporate citizenship, and brand reputation, none of which can be considered ordinary business," Trinity Br. 39, and the focus is on the "shortcomings in Wal-Mart's corporate governance and oversight over policy matters," *id.* at 33. We cannot agree. . . .

For us, the subject matter of Trinity's proposal is how Wal-Mart approaches merchandising decisions involving products that (1) especially endanger public-safety and well-being, (2) have the potential to impair the reputation of the Company, and/or (3) would reasonably be considered by many offensive to the family and community values integral to the company's promotion of the brand. A contrary holding— that the proposal's subject matter is "improved corporate governance"— would allow drafters to evade Rule 14a–8(i)(7)'s reach by styling their proposals as requesting board oversight or review. *See* Reply Br. 10. We decline to go in that direction.

2. Does Wal-Mart's approach to whether it sells particular products relate to its ordinary business operations?

A retailer's approach to its product offerings is the bread and butter of its business. As *amicus* the National Association of Manufacturers notes, "Product selection is a complicated task influenced by economic trends, data analytics, demographics, customer preferences, supply chain flexibility, shipping costs and lead-times, and a host of other factors best left to companies' management and boards of directors." . . . Though a retailer's merchandising approach is not beyond shareholder comprehension, the particulars of that approach involve operational judgments that are ordinary-course matters.

Moreover, that the proposal doesn't direct management to stop selling a particular product or prescribe a matrix to follow is, we think, a straw man. . . . A proposal need only *relate* to a company's ordinary business to be excludable. *Cf.* 17 C.F.R. § 240.14a–8(i)(7) (exclusion is proper where a proposal deals with a matter "*relating* to the company's ordinary business operations") (emphasis added). It need not dictate any particular outcome. . . . In short, so long as the subject matter of the proposal *relates*—that is, bears on—a company's ordinary business operations, the proposal is excludable unless some other exception to the exclusion applies. . . .

B. Trinity's Proposal Does Not Focus on a Significant Policy Issue that Transcends Wal-Mart's Day-to-Day Business Operations.

As discussed above, there is a significant social policy exception to the default rule of excludability for proposals that relate to a company's ordinary business operations. For the SEC staff this means that when "a proposal's underlying subject matter transcends the day-to-day business matters of the company and raises policy issues so significant that it would be appropriate for a shareholder vote, the proposal generally will not be excludable under Rule 14a–8(i)(7)." SEC Staff Legal Bulletin No. 14E . . . .

The difficulty in this case is divining the line between proposals that focus on sufficiently significant social policy issues that transcend a company's ordinary business (not excludable) from those that don't (excludable). . . .

We think the inquiry is again best split into two steps. The first is whether the proposal focuses on a significant policy (be it social or, as noted below, corporate). If it doesn't, the proposal fails to fit within the social-policy exception to Rule 14a–8(i)(7)'s exclusion. If it does, we reach the second step and ask whether the significant policy issue transcends the company's ordinary business operations.

1.   Does Trinity's proposal raise a significant social policy issue?

. . . Trinity concedes its proposal "is not directed solely to Wal-Mart's sale of guns." Trinity Mot. for Summ. J. . . . Rather it asks Wal-Mart's Board to oversee merchandising decisions for *all* "products especially dangerous to reputation, brand value, or the community that a family retailer such as Wal-Mart should carefully consider whether or not to sell." . . .

[I]t is hard to counter that Trinity's proposal doesn't touch the bases of what are significant concerns in our society and corporations in that society. Thus we deem that its proposal raises a matter of sufficiently significant policy. . . .

We are . . . persuaded . . . that, because the proposal relates to a policy issue that targets the retailer-consumer interaction, it doesn't raise an issue that *transcends* in this instance Wal-Mart's ordinary business operations, as product selection is the foundation of retail management.

2.   Even if Trinity's proposal raises a significant policy issue, does that issue transcend Wal-Mart's ordinary business operations?

. . . [T]o shield its proposal from the ordinary business exclusion, a shareholder must do more than focus its proposal on a significant policy issue; the subject matter of its proposal must "transcend" the company's ordinary business. . . . *See* 1998 Adopting Release . . .

For major retailers of myriad products, a policy issue is rarely transcendent if it treads on the meat of management's responsibility: crafting a product mix that satisfies consumer demand. This explains why the Commission's staff, almost as a matter of course, allows retailers to exclude proposals that "concern[ ] the sale of particular products and services." *Rite Aid Corp.*, SEC No-Action Letter, 2015 SEC No-Act.

LEXIS 296, 2015 WL 364996, at *1 (Mar. 24, 2015). On the other hand, if a significant policy issue disengages from the core of a retailer's business (deciding whether to sell certain goods that customers want), it is more likely to transcend its daily business dealings.

To illustrate the distinction, a proposal that asks a supermarket chain to evaluate its sale of sugary sodas because of the effect on childhood obesity should be excludable because, although the proposal raises a significant social policy issue, the request is too entwined with the fundamentals of the daily activities of a supermarket running its business: deciding which food products will occupy its shelves. So too would a proposal that, out of concern for animal welfare, aims to limit which food items a grocer sells. . . .

By contrast, a proposal raising the impropriety of a supermarket's discriminatory hiring or compensation practices generally is not excludable because, even though human resources management is a core business function, it is disengaged from the essence of a supermarket's business. *See Wal-Mart Stores, Inc.*, SEC No-Action Letter, 2004 SEC No-Act. LEXIS 298, 2004 WL 326494, at *1 (Feb. 17, 2004) (denying no-action relief where proposal asked for a report documenting "the distribution of [ ] equity compensation by the recipient's race and gender and discuss[ing] recent trends in equity compensation granted to women and employees of color"). . . .

For further support of the view that a policy issue does not transcend a company's ordinary business operations where it targets day-to-day decision-making, we look to the difference in treatment of stop-selling proposals sent to retailers and those sent to pure-play manufacturers. A policy matter relating to a product is far more likely to transcend a company's ordinary business operations when the product is that of a manufacturer with a narrow line. Here the staff often will decline a no-action request. *See, e.g., Philip Morris Companies, Inc.*, SEC No-Action Letter, 1990 SEC No-Act. LEXIS 335, 1990 WL 286063, at *1 (Feb. 22, 1990) (denying no-action relief as to proposal that requests the Board to amend the company's charter to provide that it "shall not conduct any business in tobacco or tobacco products") . . .

But the outcome changes where those same policy proposals are directed at retailers who sell thousands of products. . . . *Walgreen Co.*, SEC No-Action Letter, 1997 SEC No-Act. LEXIS 907, 1997 WL 599903, at *1 (Sept. 29, 1997) (same for proposal requesting that Walgreen stop the sale of tobacco in its stores, as it "is directed at matters relating to the conduct of the Company's ordinary business operations (i.e., the sale of a particular product)").

The reason for the difference, in our view, is that a manufacturer with a very narrow product focus—like a tobacco or gun manufacturer—exists principally to sell the product it manufactures. Its daily business deliberations do not involve whether to continue to sell the product to which it owes its reason for being. As such, a stop-selling proposal generally isn't excludable because it relates to the seller's very existence. Quite the contrary for retailers. They typically deal with thousands of products amid many options for each, precisely the sort of business decisions a retailer makes many times daily. Thus, and in contrast to the manufacturing context, a stop-selling proposal implicates a retailer's ordinary business operations and is in turn excludable. Although Trinity's proposal is not strictly a stop-selling proposal, it still targets the same basic business decision: how to weigh safety risks in the merchandising calculus.

Trinity's claim that its proposal raises a "significant" and "transcendent" *corporate* policy is likewise insufficient to fit that proposal within the social-policy exception to exclusion. See Trinity Br. 47. The relevant question to us is whether Wal-Mart's consideration of the risk that certain products pose to its "economic success" and "reputation for good corporate citizenship" is enmeshed with the way it runs its business and the retailer-consumer interaction. We think the answer is yes. Decisions relating to what products Wal-Mart sells in its rural locations versus its urban sites will vary considerably, and these are quintessentially calls made by management. Wal-Mart serves different Americas with different values. Its customers in rural America want different products than its customers in cities, and that management decides how to deal with these differing desires is not an issue typical for its Board of Directors. . . . And whether to put emphasis on brand integrity and brand protection, or none at all, is naturally a decision shareholders as well as directors entrust management to make in the exercise of their experience and business judgment.

. . .

We thus hold that, even if Trinity's proposal raises sufficiently significant social and corporate policy issues, those policies do not transcend the ordinary business operations of Wal-Mart. For a policy issue here to transcend Wal-Mart's business operations, it must target something more than the choosing of one among tens of thousands of products it sells. Trinity's proposal fails that test and is properly excludable under Rule 14a–8(i)(7). . . .

■ SHWARTZ, CIRCUIT JUDGE, with whom JUDGE VANASKIE joins as to Part III, concurring in the judgment.

. . .

The 1998 Adopting Release provides that, to avoid running afoul of the ordinary business exclusion, a proposal "relating to" a company's ordinary business must "focus[ ] on" a "sufficiently significant social policy issue." 1998 Adopting Release, 1998 SEC LEXIS 1001, 1998 WL 254809, at *4. If it does, "it generally would not be considered excludable, because the proposal[ ] would transcend . . . day-to-day business matters." *Id.* As this passage makes clear, whether a proposal focuses on an issue of social policy that is sufficiently significant is not separate and distinct from whether the proposal transcends a company's ordinary business. Rather, a proposal is sufficiently significant "because" it transcends day-to-day business matters. *Id.* Thus, the SEC treats the significance and transcendence concepts as interrelated, rather than independent.

. . . Thus, to "transcend" ordinary business, as that term is used in the 1998 Adopting Release, a proposal need not be divorced from ordinary business, as the Majority proposes, but instead must focus on a policy issue that in some "transcend[ent]" way trumps ordinary business in importance. . . .

The Majority's test, insofar as it practically gives companies carte blanche to exclude any proposal raising social policy issues that are directly related to core business operations, undermines the principle of fair corporate suffrage animating Rule 14a–8: shareholders' "ability to exercise their right—some would say their duty—to control the important decisions which affect them in their capacity as . . . owners of [a] corporation." *Med. Comm. for Human Rights v. SEC*, 432 F.2d 659, 681–82, 139 U.S. App. D.C. 226 (D.C. Cir. 1970) (footnote omitted). Section 14(a) of the Exchange Act ensures that "[a] corporation is run for the benefit of its stockholders and not for that of its managers," *SEC v. Transamerica Corp.*, 163 F.2d 511, 517 (3d Cir. 1947), and "Congress intended by its enactment of [§] 14 . . . to give true vitality to the concept of corporate democracy," *Med. Comm. for Human Rights,* 432 F.2d at 676. Permitting shareholders to vote on important social issues, including those that may be closely related to a company's ordinary business, is consistent with these principles, and I would not interpret the ordinary business exclusion to prohibit it.

II

All that said, Trinity's proposal as written is excludable under the ordinary business exclusion because it lacks the focus needed to trigger the "significant social policy" exception. To qualify for this exception, Trinity's proposal must focus on a significant policy issue. Trinity's proposal asks the Board to amend the Committee charter to require that it create policies and standards for determining whether Wal-Mart should sell a product that: (1) "especially endangers public safety and well-being"; (2) "has the substantial potential to impair" Wal-Mart's reputation; and/or (3) "would reasonably be considered by many to be offensive to the family and community values integral to" Wal-Mart's brand. . . .

The proposal has three separate components. The "public safety" component of the proposal could cover many products, especially in light of the amount of products Wal-Mart offers, and thus might require Wal-Mart to develop policies and standards for thousands of goods. While Wal-Mart's sale of guns with high-capacity magazines may raise a significant social policy issue concerning public safety, not all products that may fall within the proposal do so. Thus, while the first component of Trinity's proposal may raise a significant issue of social policy, insofar as it touches on the sale of guns equipped with high capacity magazines, we cannot say that the proposal as a whole "focus[es] on" such an issue. . . . Accordingly, Trinity may not avail itself of the "significant social policy exception" to the ordinary business exclusion.

Similarly, the second and third components of the proposal could cover many products. They are also problematic for other reasons. The second component seeks standards for determining whether Wal-Mart should sell a product that may impair the company's reputation. How Wal-Mart would like others to view it is a unique company interest, and while certainly important to shareholders seeking a return on their investment, it is not of broad societal concern. The third component, which asks the Board to consider whether the sale of a product would impact its brand, also focuses on matters of interest to the company but not society at large. Thus, these components cover matters relating to Wal-Mart's ordinary business operations, do not present a social policy issue, and render the entire proposal excludable.

III

There is an additional problem with the third component of the proposal: it is vague and thus excludable under Rule 14a–8(i)(3). Rule 14a–8(i)(3) permits a company to exclude shareholder proposals that are "so vague and ambiguous that the issuer and security holders would not be able to determine what action the proposal is contemplating," 1982 Proposing Release, 1982 SEC LEXIS 691, 1982 WL 600869, at *13. . . .

IV

I therefore concur in the judgment.

* * *

SEC Staff Legal Bulletin 14H was issued after *Trinity Wall Street*. The staff of the SEC disagreed with the Third Circuit's approach. The staff stated that, notwithstanding the holding in *Trinity Wall Street*, it will continue to follow its continuing practice that coincides with the approach taken in the concurring opinion. Recall that the SEC also believed the proposal could be omitted and thus granted Wal-Mart a no-action letter.

The Staff Legal Bulletin also addressed how to interpret Rule 14a–8(i)(9) that provides a proposal is excludable if it directly conflicts with one of the company's own proposals to be submitted to the shareholders at the same meeting. Under the test set forth in the Bulletin a conflict exists if the reasonable shareholder could not logically vote in favor of both proposals. How should the SEC rule if the shareholder proposes that the CEO cannot also be the board chair and the board is proposing the board chair should be the CEO? What if the shareholder proposal is that a holder or holders of 3 percent of the voting stock can nominate up to 3 members of the board of directors in opposition of management's bylaw proposal that limits any shareholder nomination of directors to a holder or holders of 5 percent of the company's voting shares?

NOTE ON "SETTLEMENTS" OF SHAREHOLDER PROPOSALS

Over the past few decades there has been not only a rise in the number of social and environmental proposals but a significant increase in the number of those proposals that ultimately were withdrawn because of a settlement reached between the proponent and the company. Bauer, et. al., Who Withdraws Shareholder Proposals and Does it Matter? An Analysis of Sponsor identity and Pay Practices, 23 Corp. Governance 472, 477 tbl. 1 (2015). Such settlements typically take the form of a memorandum of understanding that sets forth what the company has agreed to do in exchange for the proposal's withdrawal; the settlements are private, not public documents, being neither published by the company nor circulated among its stockholders.

> Settlement agreements on corporate campaign finance disclosure have become commonplace at large, publicly held U.S. companies. The CPA [Center of Political Accountability, a nonprofit that has taken a leading role in coordinating shareholder activism on campaign finance disclosures] has reported the existence of 141 agreements that set political spending and campaign finance disclosure practices at a major U.S. company; ISS reported that at least eleven proposals on political spending disclosure were withdrawn at U.S. companies in 2014. That year was the most successful year yet for political spending proposals that reached a shareholder vote. . . . Perhaps in reaction to this success, in 2015, at least twenty public companies were reported to settle proposals on campaign finance disclosure. Thus, in the two years from 2014 to 2015, at least thirty-one proposal settlements set campaign finance disclosure standards at U.S. public companies.

Sarah C. Haan, Shareholder Proposal Settlements and the Private Ordering of Private Elections, 126 Yale L. J. 262 (2016). Are such settlements a win-win situation for the proponent and the company?

CHAPTER 7

PERSONAL LIABILITY IN A CORPORATE CONTEXT

4. THE CORPORATE ENTITY AND THE INTERPRETATION OF STATUTES AND CONTRACTS

Page 431.[1] Add the following after Note on Interpretation:

NOTE ON THE CORPORATION'S FAITH

The Religious Freedom Restoration Act (RFRA) prohibits the "Government [from] substantially burden[ing] a person's exercise of religion" unless the Government "demonstrates that application of the burden to the person (1) is in furtherance of a compelling governmental interest; and (2) is the least restrictive means of furthering that compelling governmental interest." *Burwell v. Hobby Lobby Stores, Inc.*, 134 S. Ct. 2751 (2014), held that Hobby Lobby Stores, Inc.'s rights under the RFRA were violated by provisions of the Patient Protection and Affordable Care Act (ACA) that required employers with 50 or more full-time employees to provide health care that included providing a menu of contraceptive coverage. Hobby Lobby had about 500 stores and 13,000 employees. It was owned by five members of the Green family. Each family member had signed a pledge to run the business in accordance with the family's religious beliefs as well as to use family assets to support Christian ministries. The Greens believe that life begins at conception and that it violated their religion to facilitate access to contraceptive drugs or devices that operate after that point. They specifically objected to four methods of contraception mandated by the ACA.

The majority opinion holds that "person" as used in the RFRA includes corporations. This point was to some extent conceded by the Department of Health and Human Services which had earlier decided to provide faith-based exemptions to non-profit corporations on a case-by-case basis. The majority supported its conclusion by the Act including corporations among those deemed a "person." From this foundation it was, for the majority, axiomatic that because the RFRA accorded protection to a "person's" faith that a corporation, even one for profit, could have a faith protected by the RFRA. In reaching this conclusion, the majority emphasized that Hobby Lobby was a close corporation "owned and controlled by members of a single family, and no one has disputed the sincerity of their religious beliefs." The majority further found that the RFRA other requirements, listed above, were also met so that the ACA could not be applied to require Hobby Lobby to provide the contraceptive coverages it objected.

---

[1]   Page 315 of Concise edition.

CHAPTER 8

THE SPECIAL PROBLEMS OF SHAREHOLDERS IN CLOSE CORPORATIONS

8. CUSTODIANS AND PROVISIONAL DIRECTORS

Page 542.[1] Substitute the following case for *Giuricich v. Emtrol Corp.*:

Shawe v. Elting
Supreme Court of Delaware, 2017.
2017 Del. LEXIS 62.

■ SEITZ, JUSTICE, for the Majority:

Philip Shawe and his mother, Shirley Shawe, have filed an interlocutory appeal from the Court of Chancery's August 13, 2015 opinion and July 18, 2016 order, and related orders, appointing a custodian under 8 *Del. C.* § 226 to sell TransPerfect Global, Inc., a Delaware corporation. . . .

On appeal, the Shawes do not challenge the Court of Chancery's many factual findings of serious dysfunction and deadlock. Instead, Philip Shawe claims for the first time on appeal that the court exceeded its statutory authority when it ordered the custodian to sell a solvent company. Alternatively, Shawe contends that less drastic measures were available to address the deadlock. . . .

We disagree with the Shawes and affirm the Court of Chancery's judgment. . . .

I.

TransPerfect Global, Inc. ("TPG") is a Delaware corporation that acts as a holding company for the main operating company, TransPerfect Translations International, Inc. ("TPI"), a New York corporation. Both entities will be referred to as the "Company." The Company provides translation, website localization, and litigation support services from 92 offices in 86 worldwide cities. It has over 3,500 full-time employees and maintains a network of over 10,000 translators, editors, and proofreaders in about 170 different languages. Elting and Shawe co-founded the Company and are co-chief executive officers and board members.

TPG has 100 shares of common stock issued and outstanding, divided fifty shares to Elting, forty-nine shares to Shawe, and one share

---

[1]   Page 402 in Concise edition.

to Shirley Shawe. In this Opinion, we refer to Philip Shawe as "Shawe," and Shirley Shawe by her full name. The one share allocated to Shirley Shawe allowed TPG to claim the benefits of being a majority women-owned business. We credit the Court of Chancery's finding, based on evidence introduced at trial, that Shawe "has treated his mother's share as his own property and himself as a 50% co-owner of the Company."[1]

After a corporate reorganization in 2007, TPG's bylaws provided for a three member board of directors, or a different number fixed by the stockholders. Elting and Shawe have been the only directors since the Company's reorganization in 2007.

To fully appreciate the personal nature of the long-running discord leading to the Court of Chancery's ruling, we go back to the Company's founding and the troubled romantic relationship between the founders. Elting and Shawe co-founded the business in 1992 while living together in a dormitory room attending New York University's business school. They were engaged in 1996, but Elting called the marriage off in 1997. As the Court of Chancery found, "Shawe did not take the break-up well, and would 'terrorize' her and say 'horrendous things' about her husband, Michael Burlant, whom she married in 1999." On two separate occasions, Shawe responded to the rejection by crawling under Elting's bed and refusing to leave.[3]

As the Company grew, the founders were not satisfied with their financial success, and brought their simmering personal discontent into the Company's business affairs. The Court of Chancery catalogued the serious clashes over the years between Shawe and Elting and their surrogates before, and remarkably, during the litigation:

- Shawe engaged in a secret campaign to spy on Elting and invade her privacy by intercepting her mail, monitoring her phone calls, accessing her emails (including thousands of privileged communications with her counsel), and entering her locked office without permission on numerous occasions as well as sending his so-called "paralegal" there at 4:47 a.m. on another occasion.

- Shawe co-opted the services of Company advisors (*e.g.*, Gerber and Kasowitz) to assist him in advancing his personal agenda against Elting.

- Shawe unilaterally hired numerous employees to perform Shared Services functions (Accounting and Finance) and

---

[1] *In re Shawe & Elting LLC*, 2015 Del. Ch. LEXIS 211, 2015 WL 4874733, at *2 (Del. Ch. Aug. 13, 2015). Elting demonstrated at trial that Shawe held a general proxy for Mrs. Shawe's one share, and consistently held himself out as the 50% owner of TPG. *Id.*

[3] When Elting ended their engagement, Shawe refused to leave the apartment and crawled under her bed and stayed there for at least half an hour. App. to Opening Br. at 2393 (Trial Tr.). On another occasion, Elting was traveling alone in Buenos Aires looking for space to open a new office. She arrived at her hotel room to find that Shawe had showed up unannounced. When she asked him to leave, he crawled under her hotel bed and stayed there for about half an hour. *Id.*

even to work in divisions Elting managed (Chris Patten in TRI) without her knowledge or consent by creating "off book" arrangements and fabricating documents.

- Shawe sought to have Elting criminally prosecuted by referring to her as his ex-fiancée seventeen years after the fact when filing a "Domestic Incident Report" as a result of a seemingly minor altercation in her office.

- Shawe disparaged Elting and tried to marginalize her within the Company by gratuitously disseminating a memorandum (on Gerber's letterhead) to employees in her own division accusing her of collusion and financial improprieties.

- Shawe disparaged Elting publicly by unilaterally issuing a press release in the Company's name containing false and misleading statements.

These were just some of the highlights of the facts found by the Court of Chancery after a lengthy trial. The court also made detailed findings about continuous acrimonious disputes over personal and business expenses, weekly if not daily temper tantrums, and "mutual hostaging" between the founders over proposed acquisitions, stockholder distributions, employee hiring, pay and bonuses, and office locations. The court also found that Shawe bullied Elting and those aligned with her, expressing his desire to "create constant pain" for Elting until she agreed with Shawe's plans. It was common for senior officers to be drawn into their disputes, who were then abused by threatened firings, substantial fines, inappropriate emails, and by withholding compensation and promotions.

Specific to the Company's operations, the Court of Chancery heard days of testimony leading to findings that:

- Elting refused to pay litigation counsel to defend significant ongoing patent infringement litigation.

- Shawe fired real estate professionals, public relations professionals, refused to execute leases, and interfered with the Company's payroll processes.

- Shawe refused to engage in an annual expense true up, and interfered with the annual review of the Company's financials and its audit process.

- Shawe falsified corporate records to avoid review by Elting. . . .

II.

. . .

  The conflict eventually distilled down to Elting's petition under 8 *Del. C.* § 226 to declare a deadlock and appoint a custodian to sell TPG.

The court dedicated enormous resources to the dispute. It held twelve hearings, decided sixteen motions, and conducted a six-day trial. Before its final decision, the Court of Chancery took the measured step of appointing a custodian to serve as a mediator to assist Shawe and Elting to try and settle their disputes. The court also delayed its post-trial decision for two months to await the parties' ongoing efforts to resolve the controversy. After the many attempts at settlement failed, the Court of Chancery issued its 104-page decision finding that "the evidence presented at trial warrants the appointment of a custodian to sell the Company to resolve the deadlocks between Shawe and Elting."

First, the Court of Chancery found that Elting had satisfied the requirements of § 226(a)(1) to appoint a custodian for stockholder deadlock because the parties stipulated that they were divided and unable to elect successor directors. Next, the court held that Elting satisfied the three requirements of § 226(a)(2) for appointment of a custodian due to director deadlock. As to the first requirement, the existence of deadlocks, the court reviewed in painstaking detail its many factual findings, now undisputed on appeal, supporting its conclusion that the distrust Shawe and Elting have for each other "strikes at the heart of the palpable dysfunction that exists in the governance of the Company."

The Court of Chancery also held that the second requirement, the stockholders' inability to break the director deadlock, was satisfied by the parties' stipulation of deadlock.

Turning to the final requirement, harm to the business, the Court of Chancery considered the profitability of the Company, but also made the commonsense observation that the statute contemplates appointment of custodians for profitable corporations which, like distressed companies, can suffer or be threatened with irreparable injury. The court then catalogued some of the many examples of actual and threatened irreparable injury to the Company:

- Kevin Obarski (Senior Vice President of Sales) called the feud the "biggest business issue" the Company faces, and bemoaned that the "crazy arbitrary stuff" coming out of it was "the number 1 reason people leave to go to work at competitors."

- Michael Sank (Vice President of Corporate Development) agreed: "it's so obviously the biggest problem the company faces."

- Yu-Kai Ng (Chief Information Officer) identified as a Company goal in the wake of the 2013 Avengers meeting the need to find a way for Shawe and Elting to work together "without negatively impacting everyone else."

- Mark Hagerty (Chief Technology Officer) testified that the conflict "hurts company morale" and "is detrimental to the company."

- Robert DeNoia (former Vice President of Human Resources) expressed his frustration with the "pervasive and continuous hostile environment where inappropriate behavior impacts the morale, health and well-being of myself and the staff."

- Roy Trujillo (Chief Operating Officer), in a letter drafted for submission to a special master appointed in the New York action, attributed the "mass exodus" in Accounting and Finance to "the ongoing disputes and stressful environment created by it." He further stated that "[e]mployees are resigning and leaving these departments at unprecedented rates," that "[t]he morale and retention issue will likely spread," and that "[t]he company's reputation is taking a beating, internally and externally."

- Kai Chu (an Accounting employee), attributed the "plummeting" morale and loss of employees in Accounting to the "diametrically opposed" orders that had been received from Shawe and Elting.

- Fiona Asmah (a Finance employee) testified that the disputes and conflicting directives have caused her and others to feel "caught in the middle," have created an "unhealthy work environment," and have "affected employee morale."

Shawe himself acknowledged "the potential for grievously harming" the Company by his continued feuding with Elting.

The Court of Chancery also found that major clients who are free to use competitive services have expressed concerns about the dispute. Shawe and Elting have also been unable to agree on acquisitions which generally accounted for between 16.5–20% of the Company's annual revenue and 8–14% of its annual net profit. The Company has made no acquisitions since 2013. As the Court of Chancery held:

> [A]lthough it is true that the Company is and has been a profitable enterprise to date, its governance structure is irretrievably dysfunctional. The Company already has suffered from this dysfunction and, in my view, is threatened with much more grievous harm to its long-term prospects if the dysfunction is not addressed.

When it came to the scope of the custodian's authority, the Court of Chancery considered three alternatives. First, the court could do nothing and "leave the parties to their own devices." The court rejected this option because the "management of the Company is one of complete and utter dysfunction that is causing the business to suffer and threatens it with irreparable harm notwithstanding its profitability to date." The Chancellor "found Elting's distrust of Shawe to be justified" and "Shawe's actions have cast a pall on the prospect that a third party would pay a fair price for her shares." The court thus decided against the "do nothing" option because "equity will not suffer a wrong without a remedy."

Second, the court considered whether to appoint a custodian to serve as a third director or act in some capacity to break the ties between the two factions. He rejected this option because:

> [I]t would enmesh an outsider and, by extension, the Court into matters of internal corporate governance for an extensive period of time. Shawe and Elting are both relatively young. Absent a separation, their tenure as directors and co-CEO's of the Company could continue for decades. It is not sensible for the Court to exercise essentially perpetual oversight over the internal affairs of the Company.

This left the Court of Chancery with a final option—"appoint a custodian to sell the Company so that Shawe and Elting can be separated and the enterprise can be protected from their dysfunctional relationship." The court recognized that the remedy was "unusual," and "should be implemented only as a last resort and with extreme caution." . . .

III. . . .

A.

The statute, 8 *Del. C.* § 226(a), provides that "[t]he Court of Chancery, upon application of any stockholder, may appoint 1 or more persons to be custodians, and, if the corporation is insolvent, to be receivers, of and for any corporation [ ]." As this prefatory language contemplates, custodians are appointed for solvent corporations, and receivers are appointed for insolvent corporations.

There are three pathways to appoint a custodian for a solvent corporation, two of which are relevant to this case. First, a custodian may be appointed when:

> (1) At any meeting held for the election of directors the stockholders are so divided that they have failed to elect successors to directors whose terms have expired or would have expired upon qualification of their successors . . . .[23]

Or, a custodian may also be appointed when:

> (2) The business of the corporation is suffering or is threatened with irreparable injury because the directors are so divided respecting the management of the affairs of the corporation that the required vote for action by the board of directors cannot be

---

[23]   8 *Del. C.* § 226(a)(1).

obtained and the stockholders are unable to terminate this division . . . .[24]

Shawe does not contest the Court of Chancery's ruling that a custodian may be appointed under § 226(a)(1) due to the stockholder deadlock between Shawe and Elting, and their inability to elect successor directors. Nor could he. Shawe and Elting stipulated to the stockholder deadlock required by the statute.

Shawe does challenge the Court of Chancery's appointment of a custodian under § 226(a)(2), claiming that the court misapplied the requirement that the court find irreparable injury to the business of the corporation. According to Shawe, the court improperly relied on case law defining irreparable injury in the temporary injunction context, instead of applying a supposedly more rigorous "imminent corporate paralysis" standard under § 226. Shawe argues that applying the wrong standard "trivializes and undermines Section 226" because judicial intervention is only permitted in "extreme circumstances."

First, the argument is academic because Shawe agreed that the Court of Chancery was authorized to appoint a custodian under § 226(a)(1). Elting need not show irreparable injury under the first part of the statute. Further, the Court of Chancery did not misapply the threatened or actual irreparable injury requirement. As the court observed, "irreparable injury" is "a familiar equitable principle" which takes into account factors like "harm to a corporation's reputation, goodwill, customer relationships, and employee morale." . . .

Far from trivializing the irreparable injury requirement, the Court of Chancery accepted the fact that the Company was profitable, but also recognized the extremely dysfunctional relationship between the founders and its effect on all of the Company's operations. If allowed to persist, the Company was likely to continue on the path of plummeting employee morale, key employee departures, customer uncertainty, damage to the Company's public reputation and goodwill, and a fundamental inability to grow the Company through acquisitions.

We will not disturb these factual findings on appeal. The trial record amply supports the Court of Chancery's finding that the deadlock and dysfunction between the founders is causing threatened and actual irreparable injury to the Company.

B.

Having decided that the Court of Chancery properly exercised its discretion under § 226 to appoint a custodian of the Company, we turn to Shawe's primary argument raised for the first time on appeal—that the custodian statute does not authorize the court to order the custodian to sell the Company over the stockholders' objection. Shawe also argues that instructing the custodian to sell the Company is an extreme remedy,

---

[24] *Id.* § 226(a)(2).

and should not have been imposed without first attempting less-drastic remedies, such as using the custodian as a third director to break the ongoing deadlocks between the founders. . . .

Section 226(b) of the statute provides that:

> A custodian appointed under this section shall have all the powers and title of a receiver appointed under § 291 of this title, but the authority of the custodian is to continue the business of the corporation, and not to liquidate its affairs and distribute its assets, except when the Court shall otherwise order, and except in cases arising under paragraph (a)(3) of this section or § 352(a)(2) of this title.[34]

. . . Under the express language of the custodian statute, the Court of Chancery has the authority to "otherwise order" the custodian to "liquidate [the Company's] affairs and distribute its assets" rather than "continue the business of the corporation." . . .

According to the dissent, even though the language "except as the Court shall otherwise order" directly modifies the phrase coming before it—"not to liquidate its affairs and distribute its assets"—and is followed by the words "and except"—the dissent argues that interpretive principles should be applied to require that the exception language be read to permit liquidation only in circumstances similar to § 226(a)(3) (corporations that have abandoned their business) and § 352(a)(3) (custodians for close corporations).

The problems with this interpretation of the statute are apparent. The dissent attempts to change the plain meaning of the statutory language by invoking rules of statutory interpretation. But if a statute is clear and unambiguous, "the plain meaning of the statutory language controls."

This is because "[a]n unambiguous statute precludes the need for judicial interpretation."

Under a plain reading of § 226(b), the custodian has the powers of a receiver under § 291, and his duties are to continue the business unless the Court otherwise orders, and except under the special circumstances of abandoned businesses and close corporations. Rules of interpretation should not be invoked to contort the plain language of a statute in a manner inconsistent with its plain meaning.

Further, the dissent's interpretation also ignores the conjunctive words "and except." The statute cannot reasonably be read to express the three exceptions as a series of similar events. Instead, when the words "and except" are given meaning, the statute is reasonably read to list three distinct exceptions to the custodian's default duty to maintain the business—"except when the Court shall otherwise order;" and "except in

---

[34] 8 *Del. C.* § 226(b).

cases arising under paragraph (a)(3) of this section;" or "§ 352(a)(2) of this title."[42]

. . . [The dissent, questioned the authority of the Chancellor to order the sale of the parties' shares in TPG instead of ordering the custodian to dispose of the operating assets of TPI. The dissent based its argument on DGCL § 273 that expressly calls for asset sales as a remedy when two equal owners in a corporate joint venture are deadlocked. The Chancellor did observe this case "was within a whisker" of § 273. Nonetheless, the majority upheld the order to sell the owners' stock in TPG, reasoning to do otherwise would elevate form over substance and that it would be inefficient to allow the parties to retain their TPG shares for the purpose of then receiving a liquidating distribution when the operating assets of TPI were sold.]

Shawe also faults the Court of Chancery for ordering a sale instead of experimenting with less-intrusive measures. We agree with Shawe that a sale is a remedy to be employed reluctantly and cautiously, after a consideration of other options. The Court of Chancery should always consider less drastic alternatives before authorizing the custodian to sell a solvent company. But the remedy to address the deadlock is ultimately within the Court of Chancery's discretion.

The court did not abuse its discretion in this case. First, the court attempted other less intrusive measures by appointing a custodian immediately after trial ended to serve "as a mediator to assist Elting and Shawe in negotiating a resolution of their disputes." Almost three months later, after the first attempt at mediation failed, the court gave the parties another month before issuing its post-trial opinion "to afford them additional time to seek to resolve their disputes through the auspices of the mediator." The Court of Chancery was also aware of repeated efforts to resolve the dispute in New York, including settlement discussions, a mediation, and multiple sessions with a court-appointed Special Master. The Court of Chancery gave the parties every opportunity to resolve their acrimonious dispute outside the courthouse.

Further, the court considered whether to appoint a custodian "to serve as a third director or some form of tie-breaking mechanism in the governance of the Company." But the court rejected this option because:

> [I]t would enmesh an outsider, and, by extension, the Court into matters of internal corporate governance for an extensive period of time. Shawe and Elting are both relatively young. Absent a separation, their tenure as directors and co-CEOs of the Company could continue for decades. It is not sensible for the Court to exercise essentially perpetual oversight over the internal affairs of the Company.

And, although Shawe characterizes the Chancellor's remedy as extremely intrusive, the appointment of a custodian to act as a constant

---

[42] 8 *Del. C.* § 226(b).

monitor and tie-breaker—which is what would be required given the abundant record that Shawe and Elting cannot work together constructively—would itself be expensive, cumbersome, and very intrusive. Moreover, that approach would not facilitate, as the Chancellor's ruling does, the ability of the Company to capitalize on its business model in the efficient, flexible way that commerce demands. By preserving the Company as a whole in his remedy and allowing it to be owned and managed in the manner required to take advantage of evolving opportunities and to meet challenges effectively, the Chancellor's remedy also was well designed to protect the other constituencies of the Company—notably its employees—by positioning the company to succeed and thus to secure the jobs of its workforce.

The Chancellor was in the best position to assess the viability of options short of sale. Aware of the "extreme caution" that must be exercised before ordering a sale, he nonetheless determined that "the painfully obvious conclusion is that Shawe and Elting need to be separated from each other in the management of the Company. Their dysfunction must be excised to safeguard the Company."

We will not second-guess that first-hand judgment on appeal. . . .

V.

The Court of Chancery's August 13, 2015 opinion and July 18, 2016 order, and the related orders, are affirmed.

Dissent by: VALIHURA [omitted]

CHAPTER 9

LIMITED LIABILITY COMPANIES

2. LLCS AND THE DISTINCT ENTITY CONCEPT

A. THE ENTITY FEATURE AND ITS DISREGARD

Page 564.[1] Insert the following at the conclusion of the case:

A.G. Dillard, Inc. v. Stonehaus Construction, LLC

Supreme Court of Virginia, 2016.
2016 WL 3213630.

. . . A.G. Dillard sufficiently alleged a claim to pierce Stonehaus's corporate veil to reach Robert Hauser, the complaint alleged that Stonehaus had no bank account, held no assets, and had been legally insolvent since at least February 2013. It alleged that its funds had been siphoned by, among others, "its ultimate controlling Member (Robert Hauser)." A.G. Dillard claimed that Robert Hauser owed Stonehaus more than $160,000, but that Stonehaus had made no effort to collect this debt. These allegations claiming that Stonehaus had no assets and provided Robert Hauser, the person making decisions for Stonehaus, with financial benefits, imply that Stonehaus and Robert Hauser are not separate personalities. Further, the complaint implicitly alleged that considering Robert Hauser and Stonehaus as discrete parties would cause an injustice to A.G. Dillard in that it would not receive the benefit of its judgment against Stonehaus. Therefore, A.G. Dillard's complaint stated a claim to pierce Stonehaus's corporate veil to reach Robert Hauser.

Given that A.G. Dillard's complaint alleged a claim to pierce Stonehaus's corporate veil to reach Robert Hauser, we must decide whether A.G. Dillard alleged a claim to reverse pierce the corporate veils of the Related Entity Defendants through Robert Hauser. A.G. Dillard's complaint stated, "Robert Hauser (or an entity controlled by him, such as Darby Holdings LLC) is a Member and/or Manager of each of Stonehaus and each of the Related Entity Defendants." Viewed in the light most favorable to A.G. Dillard, the complaint alleges that Hauser is a member of each of the Related Entity Defendants. The complaint states that Stonehaus, allegedly controlled by Robert Hauser, and the Related Entity Defendants "do not operate as separate personalities, as evidenced by Stonehaus' admission that they advertise to the public as a single

---

[1] Page 424 in Concise edition.

entity and by its admission that the funds and employees of each entity are used as though the funds and employees of every entity." Viewing these allegations in the light most favorable to A.G. Dillard, the complaint implies that Robert Hauser, through his control over Stonehaus, also controls Stonehaus's corporate alter egos, the Related Entity Defendants. Therefore, A.G. Dillard's complaint stated a claim to reach the assets of the Related Entity Defendants by piercing Stonehaus's corporate veil to reach Robert Hauser and then reverse piercing the Related Entity Defendants' corporate veils through Robert Hauser.

Thus, the circuit court erred in granting a demurrer to Robert Hauser and the Related Entity Defendants regarding the piercing the corporate veil claim.

4. DISASSOCIATION AND DISSOLUTION

Page 591.[2] Insert the following before *In the Matter of 1545 Ocean Avenue, LLC*:

Reese v. Newman

District of Columbia Court of Appeals, 2016.
131 A.3d 880.

■ KING, SENIOR JUDGE:

Appellant, C. Allison Defoe Reese, and appellee, Nicole Newman, were co-owners of ANR Construction Management, LLC ("ANR"). Following disputes over management of the company, Newman notified Reese in writing that she intended to withdraw from, dissolve, and wind-up the LLC. Reese did not want to dissolve the LLC but preferred that Newman simply be dissociated so that Reese could continue the business herself. Newman filed an action for judicial dissolution in the Superior Court along with a number of other claims. Reese filed a counterclaim for Newman's dissociation in addition to other claims. Following a jury trial, the jury awarded Newman $19,000 on her conversion claim, and found grounds for both judicial dissolution and forced dissociation of Newman; the court, thereafter, ordered judicial dissolution of the LLC. All other claims by the parties were rejected. Reese appeals from a judgment entered on the jury verdicts, and the trial court's order of dissolution. We affirm.

. . .

Reese argues that the trial court erred when it purported to use discretion in choosing between dissolution of the LLC, as proposed by Newman, and forcing dissociation of Newman from the LLC, as proposed by Reese. Reese argues that the statute does not allow for any discretion

---

[2]   Page 448 at end of text in Concise edition.

by the court, and that, in fact, the statute mandates that the court order dissociation of Newman based on the jury's findings. We disagree.

. . . Our analysis starts with the plain language of the statute . . . .

Reese argues that the court was required to dissociate Newman from the LLC under D.C. Code § 29–806.02 (5) which reads:

> A person *shall* be dissociated as a member from a limited liability company when:
>
> . . .
>
> (5) On application by the company, the person is expelled as a member by judicial order because the person has:
>
> (A) Engaged, or is engaging, in wrongful conduct that has adversely and materially affected, or will adversely and materially affect, the company's activities and affairs;
>
> (B) Willfully or persistently committed, or is willfully and persistently committing, a material breach of the operating agreement or the person's duties or obligations under § 29–804.09; or
>
> (C) Engaged in, or is engaging, in conduct relating to the company's activities which makes it not reasonably practicable to carry on the activities with the person as a member. . . .

(emphasis added).

. . . While the introductory language of § 29–806.02 does use the word "shall"—that command is in no way directed at the trial judge. It reads, "[a] person shall be dissociated . . . when," and then goes on to recite fifteen separate circumstances describing different occasions *when a person shall be dissociated from an LLC.* That is to say, when one of the events described in subparagraphs (1) through (15) occurs, the member shall be dissociated. Subparagraph (5), however, is merely one instance for which a person *shall be dissociated*; that is, when and if a judge has ordered a member expelled because she finds that any conditions under (5)(A)–(C) have been established. In other words, the command in the introductory language is not directed at the trial judge, it is directed at all the circumstances set forth in subparagraphs (1) through (15) each of which identifies a different basis for which a member of an LLC shall be dissociated. There is nothing in the language of § 29–806.02 (5) that strips a judge of her discretion because it does not require the judge to expel the member if any of the enumerated conditions are established. In short, § 29–806.02 (5) means: when a judge has used her discretion to expel a member of an LLC by judicial order, under any of the enumerated circumstances in (5)(A)–(C), that member *shall* be dissociated.

. . .

Not only does the plain language necessitate an interpretation contrary to Reese's interpretation but additional authority persuades us as well. The District's law adopts language almost identical to the Revised Uniform Limited Liability Company Act (2013) ("RULLCA").[8] Section 602 (6) of the RULLCA is substantially mirrored in § 29–806.02 (5) of the D.C. Code. The comments to § 602 provide solid guidance: "[w]here grounds exist for both dissociation and dissolution, a court has the discretion to choose between the alternatives." RULLCA § 602 cmt. P 6 (citing *Robertson v. Jacobs Cattle Co.*, 285 Neb. 859, 830 N.W.2d 191, 201–02 (Neb. 2013)). The notion that a judge has discretion to choose between alternatives (dissociation or dissolution) when grounds for both exist bolsters our view that the language in § 29–806.02 (5) is not compulsory. Otherwise, when grounds for both dissolution and dissociation were present, dissolution would never be mandated by a court because dissociation of a member would always necessarily trump it.

In sum, we hold that § 29–806.02 (5) can only be interpreted to mean: when a judge finds that any of the events in (5)(A)–(C) have taken place, she may (*i.e.*, has discretion to) expel by judicial order a member of an LLC, and when a judge has done so the member *shall* be dissociated. Moreover, when both grounds for dissociation of a member and dissolution of the LLC exist, the trial judge has discretion to choose either alternative.

Here, the jury was asked to respond to specific interrogatories on the grounds for both dissociation and dissolution. The jury found that grounds were present for either outcome. The trial judge acknowledged that both options were on the table and then exercised her discretion in ordering that dissolution take place. We find no reason to disturb that order.

. . .

---

[8]   *Compare* D.C. Code § 29–806.02 *with* Revised Unif. Ltd. Liab. Co. Act § 602.

CHAPTER 10

THE DUTY OF CARE AND THE DUTY TO ACT IN GOOD FAITH

1. THE DUTY OF CARE

D. LIABILITY SHIELDS

Page 669.[1] Add the following at the end of the section:

In *Leal v. Meeks*, 115 A.3d 1173 (Del. 2015), the Delaware Supreme Court clarified the application of Delaware's immunity shield when damages are sought in connection with a transaction with an interested party to which the "entire fairness" standard is applied. With respect to a *non*-interested director of a corporation having an exculpatory provision in its charter, the suit must be dismissed if the plaintiff is unable to plead non-exculpated conduct on the part of such director. It is not, therefore, sufficient for the plaintiff to allege the directors acted in a grossly negligent manner in approving a self-dealing transaction.

2. THE DUTY TO ACT IN GOOD FAITH

Page 679.[2] Insert the following at the end of the section:

In *Central Laborers' Pension Fd. and Steamfitters Local 449 Pension Fd. v. Dimon*, 638 Fed. Appx. 34 (2nd Cir. 2016), the derivative suit complaint alleged that the directors of JP Morgan had over twenty years "turned a blind eye" to Ponzi scheme carried out by Bernard Madoff for which JP Morgan served as the primary banker. The Second Circuit affirmed dismissal on the ground of failure to state a *Caremark*-based claim under *Stone v. Ritter*. The court held that *Caremark* proscribes not the lack of a *reasonable* compliance system but the failure to implement *any* compliance system. The Second Circuit emphasized that *Caremark* itself proscribed "an utter failure to attempt to assure a reasonable information and reporting system exists" and *Stone* similarly specifies that the standard is breached when "directors utterly failed to implement any reporting or information system or controls." The Second Circuit relied on a parallel holding in *In re General Motors Derivative Litig.*, 2015 WL 3958724, at *14–15 (Del. Ch. June 26, 2015):

> Contentions that the Board did not receive specific types of information do not establish that the Board utterly failed to

---

[1]   Page 511 in Concise edition.
[2]   Page 520 in Concise edition.

attempt to assure a reasonable information and reporting system exists. . . .

That is short of pleading that the Board utterly failed to implement any reporting or information system or controls, sufficient to raise a reasonable doubt of the directors' good faith.

CHAPTER 11

THE DUTY OF LOYALTY

1. SELF-INTERESTED TRANSACTIONS

Page 695.[1] Insert the following at the end of the section:

Aiding-and-abetting liability has long been a fixture of both criminal and civil law. For example, one who aids and abets another's tort is a co-tortfeasor. Aiding and abetting liability also exists in corporate law. A recent example of such liability is *RBC Capital Mkts., LLC v. Jervis,* 129 A.2d 816 (Del. 2015), where the investment bank, RBC Capital, was held liable for nearly $76 million for its role is enabling directors of Rural/Metro Corporation to violate their fiduciary obligations in connection with the sale of Rural to the private equity firm, Warburg Pincus.

The case findings document that RBC was eager for the sale to Warburg to go forward so that it could generate fees for advising Rural and significant fees from Warburg by RBC for facilitating the loan that Warburg needed to complete the acquisition. Rural's special committee believed that Warburg's offer was inadequate and recommended that the Rural board not accept the offer. Rural had seven directors, although one did not vote on the sale to Warburg. Before the board meeting, RBC aligned itself with Rural's CEO, DeMino, who was also a director; DeMino was eager for the sale to Warburg to proceed as he would be continued in his position following Warburg's purchase. Another board member, Shackelton, was the managing partner of a hedge fund with a substantial ownership position in Rural who was eager to monetize its holdings in Rural through an M&A event. A third director, Davis, was under growing pressure from ISS because he served on too many corporate boards—a dozen; hence, the disappearance of Rural would reduce his board memberships and salve to some extent ISS's concerns that he was "over boarded." These facts caused the court to conclude the three each had personal circumstances that inclined them to a near-term sale of the company. The individual defendants settled, paying collectively $11.6 million.

The trial proceeded against RBC and the court found that the directors breached their fiduciary duty by failing to take reasonable steps to attain the best value for the Rural shareholders. The court also found that their breach was facilitated by RBC who, among other actions, deliberately reworked its fairness opinion to lower its appraised value of Rural so that Warburg's offer appeared to be more attractive. It also worked closely with DeMino, Shackelton and Davis in the days between

---

[1]   Page 529 of Concise edition.

the special committee's recommendation and the board meeting to win approval at the board level. Moreover, RBC was involved in the proxy statement's failure to disclose RBC's own conflicts of interest, so that Rural shareholders were denied this information when approving the sale.

Applying the following four-part test, the court held RBC liable as an aider and abettor of the directors' breaches:

    i)   the existence of a fiduciary relationship;

    ii)   the breach of the fiduciary's duty;

    iii)   knowing participation in that breach by the defendant; and

    iv)   damages proximately caused by the breach.

The court elaborated on the third element, observing "knowing participation in a board's fiduciary breach requires that the third party act with the knowledge that the conduct advocated or assisted constitutes a breach." *Id.* at 861–62. The Supreme Court reviewed the multiple facts supporting the trial court's finding that RBC acted with the requisite scienter:

> RBC knowingly induced the breach by exploiting its own conflicted interests to the detriment of Rural and by creating an informational vacuum.[174] RBC's knowing participation included its failure to disclose its interest in obtaining a financing role in the EMS transaction and how it planned to use its engagement as Rural's advisor to capture buy-side financing work from bidders for EMS; its knowledge that the Board and Special Committee were uninformed about Rural's value; and its failure to disclose to the Board its interest in providing the winning bidder in the Rural process with buy-side financing and its eleventh-hour attempts to secure that role while simultaneously leading the negotiations on price. RBC's desire for Warburg's business also manifested itself in its financial analysis, provided by RBC the day the Board approved the merger. RBC's illicit manipulation of the Board's deliberative processes for self-interested purposes was enabled, in part, by the Board's own lack of oversight, affording RBC "the opportunity to indulge in the misconduct which occurred." The Board was unaware of RBC's modifications to the valuation analysis, back-channel communications with Warburg, and eleventh-hour attempt to capture at least a portion of the acquirer's buy-side financing business. RBC made no effort to advise the Rural directors about these contextually shaping points. The result was a poorly-timed sale at a price that was not the product of

---

[174] *Cf. Encite LLC v. Soni*, 2011 Del. Ch. LEXIS 177, 2011 WL 5920896, at *26 (Del. Ch. Nov. 28, 2011) (recognizing that a "plaintiff can prove knowing participation by showing that a [third party] 'attempt[ed] to create or exploit conflicts of interest in the board' or 'conspire[d] in or agree[d] to the fiduciary breach' ") (citation omitted).

appropriate efforts to obtain the best value reasonably available and, as the trial court found, a failure to recognize that Rural's stand-alone value exceeded the sale price.

Id. at 863–64.

4. COMPENSATION

Page 733.[2] Insert the following case before Internal Revenue Code § 161(m) and Regulations Thereunder:

In re Inv'rs Bancorp, Inc. Stockholder Litig.

Supreme Court of Delaware, 2017.
177 A.3d 1208.

■ SEITZ, JUSTICE:

In this appeal we consider the limits of the stockholder ratification defense when directors make equity awards to themselves under the general parameters of an equity incentive plan. . . .

For equity incentive plans in which the award terms are fixed and the directors have no discretion how they allocate the awards, the stockholders know exactly what they are being asked to approve. But, other plans—like the equity incentive plan in this appeal—create a pool of equity awards that the directors can later award to themselves in amounts and on terms they decide. The Court of Chancery has recognized a ratification defense for such discretionary plans as long as the plan has "meaningful limits" on the awards directors can make to themselves. If the discretionary plan does not contain meaningful limits, the awards, if challenged, are subject to an entire fairness standard of review. . . .

I.

. . . The defendants fall into two groups—ten non-employee director defendants and two executive director defendants. Investors Bancorp, the nominal defendant, is a Delaware corporation with its principal place of business in Short Hills, New Jersey. Investors Bancorp is a holding company for Investors Bank, a New Jersey chartered savings bank with corporate headquarters in Short Hills, New Jersey. The Company operates 143 banking branches in New Jersey and New York. In 2014, after a mutual-to-stock conversion, Investors Bancorp conducted a second-step offering to the public, which is when the plaintiffs acquired their shares. In this second-step offering, the Company sold 219,580,695 shares and raised about $2.15 billion.

The board sets director compensation based on recommendations of the Compensation and Benefits Committee ("Committee"), composed of seven of the ten non-employee directors. . . . As the Court of Chancery noted, the annual compensation for all non-employee directors ranged

---

[2]   Page 559 of the Concise edition.

from $97,200 to $207,005, with $133,340 as the average amount of compensation per director . . . .

In 2014, Cummings, the Company's President and CEO, received (i) a $1,000,000 base salary; (ii) an Annual Cash Incentive Award of up to 150% of his base salary contingent on certain performance goals; and (iii) perquisites and benefits valued at $278,400, which totaled $2,778,700. Cama, the Company's COO and Senior Executive Vice President, received annual compensation consisting of (i) a $675,000 base salary; (ii) an Annual Cash Incentive Award of up to 120% of his base salary; and (iii) perquisites and benefits valued at $180,794, which totaled $1,665,794.

At the end of 2014, following completion of the conversion plan, the Committee met to review 2014 director compensation and set compensation for 2015. Gregory Keshishian, a compensation consultant from GK Partners, Inc., presented to the board a study of director compensation for eighteen publicly held peer companies. According to the study, these companies paid their non-employee directors an average of $157,350 in total compensation. The Company's $133,340 average non-employee director compensation in 2014 fell close to the study average. Following the presentation, the Committee recommended to the board that the non-employee director compensation package remain the same for 2015. . . .

The Committee also reviewed the compensation package for executive officers. After GK Partners reviewed peer-average figures with the committee, the committee unanimously recommended no changes to Cummings' or Cama's annual salary, but recommended an increase in the 2015 Annual Cash Incentive Award from 150% to 200%, and 120% to 160% of their base salaries, respectively. . . .

Just a few months after setting the 2015 board compensation, in March, 2015, the board proposed the 2015 EIP. The EIP was intended to "provide additional incentives for [the Company's] officers, employees and directors to promote [the Company's] growth and performance and to further align their interests with those of [the Company's] stockholders . . . and give [the Company] the flexibility [needed] to continue to attract, motivate and retain highly qualified officers, employees and directors."

The Company reserved 30,881,296 common shares for restricted stock awards, restricted stock units, incentive stock options, and non-qualified stock options for the Company's 1,800 officers, employees, non-employee directors, and service providers. The EIP has limits within each category. Of the total shares, a maximum of 17,646,455 can be issued for stock options or restricted stock awards and 13,234,841 for restricted stock units or performance shares. Those limits are further broken down for employee and non-employee directors:

- A maximum of 4,411,613 shares, in the aggregate (25% of the shares available for stock option awards), may be issued or delivered to any one employee pursuant to the exercise of stock options;

- A maximum of 3,308,710 shares, in the aggregate (25% of the shares available for restricted stock awards and restricted stock units), may be issued or delivered to any one employee as a restricted stock or restricted stock unit grant; and

- The maximum number of shares that may be issued or delivered to all non-employee directors, in the aggregate, pursuant to the exercise of stock options or grants of restricted stock or restricted stock units shall be 30% of all option or restricted stock shares available for awards, "all of which may be granted in any calendar year."

- According to the proxy sent to stockholders, "[t]he number, types and terms of awards to be made pursuant to the [EIP] are subject to the discretion of the Committee and have not been determined at this time, and will not be determined until subsequent to stockholder approval." At the Company's June 9, 2015 annual meeting, 96.25% of the voting shares approved the EIP (79.1% of the total shares outstanding).

    . . . [In the ensuing two weeks, the Committee held four meetings that resulted in the Committee approving awards of restricted stock and stock options to all board members. According to the complaint, these awards were not part of the final 2015 compensation package nor discussed in any prior meetings. The Committee was advised by its outside counsel and relied heavily on its compensation consultant Keshishian; central to their decision was a list of the stock options and awards granted by the 164 companies that underwent mutual-to-stock conversions in the then preceding twenty years. The complaint, however, alleged that the list did not compare five other companies on the list that met the criteria and had more recently undergone conversions—each of which granted significantly lower awards. At the fourth meeting, the directors awarded themselves 7.8 million shares. Non-employee directors each received 250,000 stock options—valued at $780,000—and 100,000 restricted shares—valued at $1,254,000. Peer companies' non-employee awards averaged $175,817. Cummings received 1,333,333 stock options and 1,000,000 restricted shares, valued at $16,699,999 and alleged to be 1,759% higher than the peer companies' average compensation for executive directors. Cama received 1,066,666 stock options and 600,000 restricted shares, valued at $13,359,998 and alleged to be 2,571% higher than the peer companies' average. According to the complaint, the total fair value of the awards was $51,653,997. . . .]

After the Company disclosed the awards, stockholders filed three separate complaints in the Court of Chancery alleging breaches of fiduciary duty by the directors for awarding themselves excessive compensation. . . .

The Court of Chancery . . . dismissed the plaintiffs' complaint . . . [on the grounds] the EIP contained "meaningful, specific limits on awards to all director beneficiaries" . . . . We review the Court of Chancery decision dismissing the complaint *de novo*.

II.

Unless restricted by the certificate of incorporation or bylaws, Section 141(h) of Delaware General Corporation Law ("DGCL") authorizes the board "to fix the compensation of directors." Although authorized to do so by statute, when the board fixes its compensation, it is self-interested in the decision because the directors are deciding how much they should reward themselves for board service. If no other factors are involved, the board's decision will "lie outside the business judgment rule's presumptive protection, so that, where properly challenged, the receipt of self-determined benefits is subject to an affirmative showing that the compensation arrangements are fair to the corporation." In other words, the entire fairness standard of review will apply.

Other factors do sometimes come into play. When a fully informed, uncoerced, and disinterested majority of stockholders approve the board's authorized corporate action, the stockholders are said to have ratified the corporate act. Stockholder ratification of corporate acts applies in different corporate law settings. Here, we address the affirmative defense of stockholder ratification of director self-compensation decisions. . . .

III.

A.

As ratification has evolved for stockholder-approved equity incentive plans, the courts have recognized the defense in three situations—when stockholders approved the specific director awards; when the plan was self-executing, meaning the directors had no discretion when making the awards; or when directors exercised discretion and determined the amounts and terms of the awards after stockholder approval. The first two scenarios present no real problems. When stockholders know precisely what they are approving, ratification will generally apply. The rub comes, however, in the third scenario, when directors retain discretion to make awards under the general parameters of equity incentive plans. . . .

We think . . . when it comes to the discretion directors exercise following stockholder approval of an equity incentive plan, ratification cannot be used to foreclose the Court of Chancery from reviewing those further discretionary actions when a breach of fiduciary duty claim has been properly alleged. As the Court of Chancery emphasized in *Sample[v. Morgan*, 914 A.2d 647 (Del. Ch. 2007)], using an expression coined many years ago, director action is "twice-tested," first for legal authorization, and second by equity.[81] When stockholders approve the general parameters of an equity compensation plan and allow directors to exercise their "broad legal authority" under the plan, they do so "precisely because they know that that authority must be exercised consistently with equitable principles of fiduciary duty."[82] The stockholders have granted the directors the legal authority to make awards. But, the directors' exercise of that authority must be done consistent with their fiduciary duties. Given that the actual awards are self-interested decisions not approved by the stockholders, if the directors acted inequitably when making the awards, their "inequitable action does not become permissible simply because it is legally possible"[83] under the general authority granted by the stockholders.

. . . [W]hen a stockholder properly alleges that the directors breached their fiduciary duties when exercising their discretion after stockholders approve the general parameters of an equity incentive plan, the directors should have to demonstrate that their self-interested actions were entirely fair to the company.[85]

B.

The Investors Bancorp EIP is a discretionary plan as described above. It covers about 1,800 officers, employees, non-employee directors, and service providers. Specific to the directors, the plan reserves 30,881,296 shares of common stock for restricted stock awards, restricted stock units, incentive stock options, and non-qualified stock options for the Company's officers, employees, non-employee directors, and service providers. Of those reserved shares and other equity, the non-employee directors were entitled to up to 30% of all option and restricted stock shares, all of which could be granted in any calendar year. But, "[t]he number, types, and terms of the awards to be made pursuant to the [EIP] are subject to the discretion of the Committee and have not been determined at this time, and will not be determined until subsequent to stockholder approval."

When submitted to the stockholders for approval, the stockholders were told that "[b]y approving the Plan, stockholders will give [the Company] the flexibility [it] need[s] to continue to attract, motivate and retain highly qualified officers, employees and directors by offering a

---

[81] *Sample*, 914 A.2d at 672 (Strine, V.C.) (citing Adolf A. Berle, *Corporate Powers as Powers in Trust*, 44 HARV. L. REV. 1049, 1049 (1931)) ("Corporate acts thus must be 'twice-tested'—once by the law and again by equity.").

[82] *Id.* at 584.

[83] *Schnell v. Chris-Craft Ind., Inc.*, 285 A.2d 437, 439 (Del. 1971). As noted in *Desimone v. Barrows*, 924 A.2d 908, 917 (Del. Ch. 2007), "[s]pecifying the precise amount and form of director compensation . . . 'ensure[s] integrity' in the underlying principal-agent relationship between stockholders and directors."

[85] For example, in *Seinfeld* [*v. Slager*, 2012 Del. Ch. LEXIS 139 (Del. Ch. June 29, 2012)], the Court of Chancery refused to extend stockholder approval of the plan to the awards themselves. . . .The directors had the "theoretical ability to award themselves as much as tens of millions of dollars per year, with few limitations." *Id.* The board was also "free to use its absolute discretion . . . with little guidance as to the total pay that can be awarded." *Id.* . . . .

competitive compensation program that is linked to the performance of [the Company's] common stock." The complaint alleges that this representation was reasonably interpreted as forward-looking. In other words, by approving the EIP, stockholders understood that the directors would reward Company employees for future performance, not past services.

After stockholders approved the EIP, the board eventually approved just under half of the stock options available to the directors and nearly thirty percent of the shares available to the directors as restricted stock awards, based predominately on a five-year going forward vesting period. The plaintiffs argue that the directors breached their fiduciary duties by granting themselves these awards because they were unfair and excessive. According to the plaintiffs, the stockholders were told the EIP would reward future performance, but the Board instead used the EIP awards to reward past efforts for the mutual-to-stock conversion—which the directors had already accounted for in determining their 2015 compensation packages. Also, according to the plaintiffs, the rewards were inordinately higher than peer companies'. As alleged in the complaint, the Board paid each non-employee director more than $2,100,000 in 2015, which "eclips[ed] director pay at every Wall Street firm." This significantly exceeded the Company's non-employee director compensation in 2014, which ranged from $97,200 to $207,005. It also far surpassed the $198,000 median pay at similarly sized companies and the $260,000 median pay at much larger companies. And the awards were over twenty-three times more than the $87,556 median award granted to other companies' non-employee directors after mutual-to-stock conversions.

In addition, according to the complaint, Cama and Cummings' compensation far exceeded their prior compensation and that of peer companies. Cummings' $20,006,957 total compensation in 2015 was seven times more than his 2014 compensation package of $2,778,000. And Cama's $15,318,257 compensation was nine times more than his 2014 compensation package of $1,665,794. Cummings' $16,699,999 award was 3,683% higher than the median award other companies granted their CEOs after mutual-to-stock conversions. And Cama's $13,359,998 award was 5,384% higher than the median other companies granted their second-highest paid executives after the conversions.[99]

The plaintiffs have alleged facts leading to a pleading stage reasonable inference that the directors breached their fiduciary duties in making unfair and excessive discretionary awards to themselves after stockholder approval of the EIP. Because the stockholders did not ratify the specific awards the directors made under the EIP, the directors must demonstrate the fairness of the awards to the Company. . . .

---

[99] The average awards at peer companies were $898,490 for CEOs and $510,435 for the second-highest paid executives. . . .

V.

The Investors Bancorp stockholders approved the general parameters of the EIP. The plaintiffs have properly alleged, however, that the directors, when exercising their discretion under the EIP, acted inequitably in granting themselves unfair and excessive awards. Because the stockholders did not ratify the specific awards under the EIP, the affirmative defense of ratification cannot not be used to dismiss the complaint. . . . Thus, the Court of Chancery's decision is reversed, and the case is remanded for further proceedings consistent with this opinion.

Page 733. Update Note on Tax Treatment of Executive Compensation with the following:

The multifaceted tax legislation enacted in late 2017 eliminated the exception for "performance-based compensation." As amended, the IRC disallows the deduction of compensation to the extent the amount paid to the CEO, the CFO, and the three most highly compensated officers (other than the CEO and CFO) exceeds $1 million per individual. The provision applies only to public companies.

6. DUTIES OF CONTROLLING SHAREHOLDERS

A. REGULATING THE EXERCISE OF CONTROL

Page 799.[3] Add the following before *Jones v. H.F. Ahmanson Company*:

NOTE ON ALTERNATIVE APPROACHES TO CHALLENGES TO TRANSACTIONS WITH CONTROLLING STOCKHOLDERS

In *Calesa Assocs., L.P. v. American Capital, Ltd.,* 2016 Del. Ch. LEXIS 41 (Del. Ch. Feb. 29, 2016), shareholders challenged a refinancing plan initiated by the holder of 26 percent of its voting stock alleging it reflected the ill effects of controlling influence over the financially floundering company. Rather than consider whether such ownership constituted control and whether under *Sinclair* the plan constituted "self-dealing," Vice-Chancellor Glasscock held the transaction was outside the presumptive protection of the business judgment rule because at least four of the six directors were not disinterested with respect to the transaction. For example, one of the directors served on the board of the 26 percent holder, another was the CEO of a company controlled by that holder, and the other two directors would themselves benefit directly from the refinancing plan. The court also reasoned that should it later conclude that the 26 percent holder was not a controlling stockholder it could be liable under a theory it aided and abetted misconduct of the directors under the four-part aiding and abetting standard set forth above in *RBC Capital*.

---

[3]   Page 606 in Concise edition.

CHAPTER 12

THE ANTIFRAUD PROVISION: SECTION 10(b) AND RULE 10b–5

4. DUTY TO SPEAK

Page 878.[1] Insert the following after Note 5:

Although the next case does not arise under Section 10(b) and Rule 10b–5, it reflects the Supreme Court's handling of the duty to disclose.

Omnicare, Inc. v. Laborers Dist. Council Constr. Indus. Pension Fund

Supreme Court of the United States, 2015.
___ U.S. ___, 135 S.Ct. 1318, 191 L.Ed.2d 253.

■ JUSTICE KAGAN delivered the opinion of the Court.

Before a company may sell securities in interstate commerce, it must file a registration statement with the Securities and Exchange Commission (SEC). If that document either "contain[s] an untrue statement of a material fact" or "omit[s] to state a material fact . . . necessary to make the statements therein not misleading," a purchaser of the stock may sue for damages. . . . This case requires us to decide how each of those phrases applies to statements of opinion.

I. . . .

Section 11 thus creates two ways to hold issuers liable for the contents of a registration statement—one focusing on what the statement says and the other on what it leaves out. Either way, the buyer need not prove (as he must to establish certain other securities offenses) that the defendant acted with any intent to deceive or defraud. *Herman & MacLean* v. *Huddleston*, 459 U.S. 375, 381–382 . . . (1983).

This case arises out of a registration statement that petitioner Omnicare filed in connection with a public offering of common stock. Omnicare is the nation's largest provider of pharmacy services for residents of nursing homes. Its registration statement contained . . . analysis of the effects of various federal and state laws on its business model, including its acceptance of rebates from pharmaceutical manufacturers. . . . Of significance here, two sentences in the registration

---

[1] Page 667 of Concise edition.

statement expressed Omnicare's view of its compliance with legal requirements:

- "We believe our contract arrangements with other healthcare providers, our pharmaceutical suppliers and our pharmacy practices are in compliance with applicable federal and state laws." . . .

- "We believe that our contracts with pharmaceutical manufacturers are legally and economically valid arrangements that bring value to the healthcare system and the patients that we serve." . . .

Accompanying those legal opinions were some caveats. On the same page as the first statement above, Omnicare mentioned several state-initiated "enforcement actions against pharmaceutical manufacturers" for offering payments to pharmacies that dispensed their products; it then cautioned that the laws relating to that practice might "be interpreted in the future in a manner inconsistent with our interpretation and application." . . . And adjacent to the second statement, Omnicare noted that the Federal Government had expressed "significant concerns" about some manufacturers' rebates to pharmacies and warned that business might suffer "if these price concessions were no longer provided." . . .

Respondents here, pension funds that purchased Omnicare stock in the public offering (hereinafter Funds), brought suit alleging that the company's two opinion statements about legal compliance give rise to liability under § 11. Citing lawsuits that the Federal Government later pressed against Omnicare, the Funds' complaint maintained that the company's receipt of payments from drug manufacturers violated anti-kickback laws. . . . Accordingly, the complaint asserted, Omnicare made "materially false" representations about legal compliance. . . . And so too, the complaint continued, the company "omitted to state [material] facts necessary" to make its representations not misleading. . . . The Funds claimed that none of Omnicare's officers and directors "possessed reasonable grounds" for thinking that the opinions offered were truthful and complete. . . . Indeed, the complaint noted that one of Omnicare's attorneys had warned that a particular contract "carrie[d] a heightened risk" of liability under anti-kickback laws. . . . At the same time, the Funds made clear that in light of § 11's strict liability standard, they chose to "exclude and disclaim any allegation that could be construed as alleging fraud or intentional or reckless misconduct." . . . .

The District Court granted Omnicare's motion to dismiss. . . . In the court's view, "statements regarding a company's belief as to its legal compliance are considered 'soft' information" and are actionable only if those who made them "knew [they] were untrue at the time." App. to Pet. for Cert. 38a. The court concluded that the Funds' complaint failed to meet that standard because it nowhere claimed that "the company's officers knew they were violating the law." *Id.*, at 39a. The Court of Appeals for the Sixth Circuit reversed. See 719 F.3d 498 (2013). It acknowledged that the two statements highlighted in the Funds' complaint expressed Omnicare's "opinion" of legal compliance, rather than "hard facts." *Id.*, at 504 .... But even so, the court held, the Funds had to allege only that the stated belief was "objectively false"; they did not need to contend that anyone at Omnicare "disbelieved [the opinion] at the time it was expressed." 719 F.3d, at 506 (quoting *Fait* v. *Regions Financial Corp.*, 655 F.3d 105, 110 (CA2 2011)).

We granted certiorari . . . to consider how § 11 pertains to statements of opinion. We do so in two steps, corresponding to the two parts of § 11 and the two theories in the Funds' complaint. We initially address the Funds' claim that Omnicare made "untrue statement[s] of . . . material fact" in offering its views on legal compliance. . . . We then take up the Funds' argument that Omnicare "omitted to state a material fact . . . necessary to make the statements [in its registration filing] not misleading." . . . Unlike both courts below, we see those allegations as presenting different issues. In resolving the first, we discuss when an opinion itself constitutes a factual misstatement. In analyzing the second, we address when an opinion may be rendered misleading by the omission of discrete factual representations. Because we find that the Court of Appeals applied the wrong standard, we vacate its decision.

II

The Sixth Circuit held, and the Funds now urge, that a statement of opinion that is ultimately found incorrect—even if believed at the time made—may count as an "untrue statement of a material fact." . . . As the Funds put the point, a statement of belief may make an implicit assertion about the belief's "subject matter": To say "we believe X is true" is often to indicate that "X is in fact true." . . . In just that way, the Funds conclude, an issuer's statement that "we believe we are following the law" conveys that "we in fact are following the law"—which is "materially false," no matter what the issuer thinks, if instead it is violating an anti-kickback statute. . . .

But that argument wrongly conflates facts and opinions. . . . Congress effectively incorporated just that distinction in § 11's first part by exposing issuers to liability not for "untrue statement[s]" full stop (which would have included ones of opinion), but only for "untrue statement[s] of . . . *fact*." § 77k(a) (emphasis added).

Consider that statutory phrase's application to two hypothetical statements, couched in ways the Funds claim are equivalent. A company's CEO states: "The TVs we manufacture have the highest resolution available on the market." Or, alternatively, the CEO transforms that factual statement into one of opinion: "I *believe*" (or "I think") "the TVs we manufacture have the highest resolution available on the market." The first version would be an untrue statement of fact if a competitor had introduced a higher resolution TV a month before—even assuming the CEO had not yet learned of the new product. The CEO's assertion, after all, is not mere puffery, but a determinate, verifiable statement about her company's TVs; and the CEO, however innocently, got the facts wrong. But in the same set of circumstances, the second version would remain true. Just as she said, the CEO really did believe, when she made the statement, that her company's TVs had the sharpest picture around. And although a plaintiff could later prove that opinion erroneous, the words "I believe" themselves admitted that possibility, thus precluding liability for an untrue statement of fact. That remains the case if the CEO's opinion, as here, concerned legal compliance. If, for example, she said, "I believe our marketing practices are lawful," and actually did think that, she could not be liable for a false statement of fact—even if she afterward discovered a longtime violation of law. Once again, the statement would have been true, because all she expressed was a view, not a certainty, about legal compliance.

That still leaves some room for § 11's false-statement provision to apply to expressions of opinion. As even Omnicare acknowledges, every such statement explicitly affirms one fact: that the speaker actually holds the stated belief. . . . For that reason, the CEO's statement about product quality ("I believe our TVs have the highest resolution available on the market") would be an untrue statement of fact—namely, the fact of her own belief—if she knew that her company's TVs only placed second. And so too the statement about legal compliance ("I believe our marketing practices are lawful") would falsely describe her own state of mind if she thought her company was breaking the law. In such cases, § 11's first part would subject the issuer to liability (assuming the misrepresentation were material). . . .

The two sentences to which the Funds object are pure statements of opinion: To simplify their content only a bit, Omnicare said in each that "we believe we are obeying the law." And the Funds do not contest that Omnicare's opinion was honestly held. Recall that their complaint explicitly "exclude[s] and disclaim[s]" any allegation sounding in fraud or deception. . . . What the Funds instead claim is that Omnicare's belief turned out to be wrong—that whatever the company thought, it was in fact violating anti-kickback laws. But that allegation alone will not give rise to liability under § 11's first clause because, as we have shown, a sincere statement of pure opinion is not an "untrue statement of material fact," regardless whether an investor can ultimately prove the belief wrong. That clause, limited as it is to factual statements, does not allow investors to second-guess inherently subjective and uncertain assessments. In other words, the provision is not, as the Court of Appeals and the Funds would have it, an invitation to Monday morning quarterback an issuer's opinions.

III

A

That conclusion, however, does not end this case because the Funds also rely on § 11's omissions provision, alleging that Omnicare "omitted to state facts necessary" to make its opinion on legal compliance "not misleading."[3] . . . We therefore must consider when, if ever, the omission of a fact can make a statement of opinion like Omnicare's, even if literally accurate, misleading to an ordinary investor.

Omnicare claims that is just not possible. On its view, no reasonable person, in any context, can understand a pure statement of opinion to convey anything more than the speaker's own mindset. . . .

That claim has more than a kernel of truth. A reasonable person understands, and takes into account, the difference we have discussed above between a statement of fact and one of opinion. See *supra*, at 6–7. She recognizes the import of words like "I think" or "I believe," and grasps that they convey some lack of certainty as to the statement's content. . . . And that may be especially so when the phrases appear in a registration statement, which the reasonable investor expects has been carefully wordsmithed to comply with the law. When reading such a document, the investor thus distinguishes between the sentences "we believe X is true" and "X is true." And because she does so, the omission of a fact that merely rebuts the latter statement fails to render the former misleading. In other words, a statement of opinion is not misleading just because external facts show the opinion to be incorrect. Reasonable investors do not understand such statements as guarantees, and § 11's omissions clause therefore does not treat them that way.

But Omnicare takes its point too far, because a reasonable investor may, depending on the circumstances, understand an opinion statement to convey facts about how the speaker has formed the opinion—or, otherwise put, about the speaker's basis for holding that view. And if the real facts are otherwise, but not provided, the opinion statement will mislead its audience. Consider an unadorned statement of opinion about legal compliance: "We believe our conduct is lawful." If the issuer makes that statement without having consulted a lawyer, it could be misleadingly incomplete. In the context of the securities market, an investor, though recognizing that legal opinions can prove wrong in the end, still likely expects such an assertion to rest on some meaningful legal inquiry—rather than, say, on mere intuition, however sincere. Similarly, if the issuer made the statement in the face of its lawyers' contrary advice, or with knowledge that the Federal Government was taking the opposite view, the investor again has cause to complain: He expects not just that the issuer believes the opinion (however irrationally), but that it fairly aligns with the information in the issuer's possession at the time.[6] Thus, if a registration statement omits material

---

[3]   Section 11's omissions clause also applies when an issuer fails to make mandated disclosures—those "required to be stated"—in a registration statement. § 77k(a). But the Funds do not object to Omnicare's filing on that score.

[6]   The hypothetical used earlier could demonstrate the same points. Suppose the CEO, in claiming that her company's TV had the highest resolution available on the market, had failed to review any of her competitors' product specifications. Or suppose she had recently received information from industry analysts indicating that a new product had surpassed her company's on this metric. The CEO may still honestly believe in her TV's superiority. But under § 11's

facts about the issuer's inquiry into or knowledge concerning a statement of opinion, and if those facts conflict with what a reasonable investor would take from the statement itself, then § 11's omissions clause creates liability.

An opinion statement, however, is not necessarily misleading when an issuer knows, but fails to disclose, some fact cutting the other way. Reasonable investors understand that opinions sometimes rest on a weighing of competing facts; indeed, the presence of such facts is one reason why an issuer may frame a statement as an opinion, thus conveying uncertainty. . . . Suppose, for example, that in stating an opinion about legal compliance, the issuer did not disclose that a single junior attorney expressed doubts about a practice's legality, when six of his more senior colleagues gave a stamp of approval. That omission would not make the statement of opinion misleading, even if the minority position ultimately proved correct: A reasonable investor does not expect that *every* fact known to an issuer supports its opinion statement.[8]

Moreover, whether an omission makes an expression of opinion misleading always depends on context. Registration statements as a class are formal documents, filed with the SEC as a legal prerequisite for selling securities to the public. Investors do not, and are right not to, expect opinions contained in those statements to reflect baseless, off-the-cuff judgments, of the kind that an individual might communicate in daily life. At the same time, an investor reads each statement within such a document, whether of fact or of opinion, in light of all its surrounding text, including hedges, disclaimers, and apparently conflicting information. . . . So an omission that renders misleading a statement of opinion when viewed in a vacuum may not do so once that statement is considered, as is appropriate, in a broader frame. The reasonable investor understands a statement of opinion in its full context, and § 11 creates liability only for the omission of material facts that cannot be squared with such a fair reading.

These principles are not unique to § 11: They inhere, too, in much common law respecting the tort of misrepresentation. The Restatement of Torts, for example, recognizes that "[a] statement of opinion as to facts not disclosed and not otherwise known to the recipient may" in some circumstances reasonably "be interpreted by him as an implied statement" that the speaker "knows facts sufficient to justify him in forming" the opinion, or that he at least knows no facts "incompatible

---

omissions provision, that subjective belief, in the absence of the expected inquiry or in the face of known contradictory evidence, would not insulate her from liability.

[8]   We note, too, that a reasonable investor generally considers the specificity of an opinion statement in making inferences about its basis. Compare two new statements from our ever-voluble CEO. In the first, she says: "I believe we have 1.3 million TVs in our warehouse." In the second, she says: "I believe we have enough supply on hand to meet demand." All else equal, a reasonable person would think that a more detailed investigation lay behind the former statement.

with [the] opinion." Restatement (Second) of Torts § 539, p. 85 (1976).[10] When that is so, the Restatement explains, liability may result from omission of facts—for example, the fact that the speaker failed to conduct any investigation—that rebut the recipient's predictable inference. See *id.*, Comment *a*, at 86; *id.*, Comment *b*, at 87 . . .

And the purpose of § 11 supports this understanding of how the omissions clause maps onto opinion statements. Congress adopted § 11 to ensure that issuers "tell[ ] the whole truth" to investors. H. R. Rep. No. 85, 73d Cong., 1st Sess., 2 (1933) (quoting President Roosevelt's message to Congress). For that reason, literal accuracy is not enough: An issuer must as well desist from misleading investors by saying one thing and holding back another. Omnicare would nullify that statutory requirement for all sentences starting with the phrases "we believe" or "we think." But those magic words can preface nearly any conclusion, and the resulting statements, as we have shown, remain perfectly capable of misleading investors. . . . Thus, Omnicare's view would punch a hole in the statute for half-truths in the form of opinion statements. . . .

According to Omnicare, any inquiry into the issuer's basis for holding an opinion is "hopelessly amorphous," threatening "unpredictable" and possibly "massive" liability. . . .

Omnicare way overstates both the looseness of the inquiry Congress has mandated and the breadth of liability that approach threatens. As we have explained, an investor cannot state a claim by alleging only that an opinion was wrong; the complaint must as well call into question the issuer's basis for offering the opinion. . . . To be specific: The investor must identify particular (and material) facts going to the basis for the issuer's opinion—facts about the inquiry the issuer did or did not conduct or the knowledge it did or did not have—whose omission makes the opinion statement at issue misleading to a reasonable person reading the statement fairly and in context. . . . That is no small task for an investor.

. . . B

Our analysis on this score counsels in favor of sending the case back to the lower courts for decision. . . . In doing so, however, we reemphasize a few crucial points pertinent to the inquiry on remand. Initially, as we have said, the Funds cannot proceed without identifying one or more facts left out of Omnicare's registration statement. . . . At oral argument . . . the Funds highlighted . . . [a] more specific allegation in their complaint: that an attorney had warned Omnicare that a particular contract "carrie[d] a heightened risk" of legal exposure under anti-kickback laws. . . . On remand, the court must review the Funds' complaint to determine whether it adequately alleged that Omnicare had omitted that (purported) fact, or any other like it, from the registration statement. And if so, the court must determine whether the omitted fact

---

[10] The Restatement [(Second)] of Contracts, [§ 168. p. 455 (1979),] discussing misrepresentations that can void an agreement, says much the same. . . .).

would have been material to a reasonable investor—*i.e.*, whether "there is a substantial likelihood that a reasonable [investor] would consider it important." *TSC Industries*, 426 U.S., at 449 . . . .

Assuming the Funds clear those hurdles, the court must ask whether the alleged omission rendered Omnicare's legal compliance opinions misleading in the way described earlier—*i.e.*, because the excluded fact shows that Omnicare lacked the basis for making those statements that a reasonable investor would expect. . . . Insofar as the omitted fact at issue is the attorney's warning, that inquiry entails consideration of such matters as the attorney's status and expertise and other legal information available to Omnicare at the time. . . . Further, the analysis of whether Omnicare's opinion is misleading must address the statement's context. . . . That means the court must take account of whatever facts Omnicare *did* provide about legal compliance, as well as any other hedges, disclaimers, or qualifications it included in its registration statement. The court should consider, for example, the information Omnicare offered that States had initiated enforcement actions against drug manufacturers for giving rebates to pharmacies, that the Federal Government had expressed concerns about the practice, and that the relevant laws "could "be interpreted in the future in a manner" that would harm Omnicare's business. . . .

With these instructions and for the reasons stated, we vacate the judgment below and remand the case for further proceedings.

It is so ordered.

■ JUSTICE SCALIA, concurring in part and concurring in the judgment. (opinion omitted).

■ JUSTICE THOMAS, concurring in the judgment. (opinion omitted)

5. PRIMARY PARTICIPANTS AFTER *CENTRAL BANK*

Page 890.[2] Insert the following after *Janus Capital Group, Inc. v. First Derivative Traders*:

West Virginia Pipe Trades Health & Welfare Fund v. Medtronic, Inc.

United States Court of Appeals, Eighth Circuit, 2016.
845 F.3d 384.

. . . Medtronic developed INFUSE as an alternative to bone grafting procedures, and the FDA approved it for use in lower back spinal fusion surgeries in 2002. [FDA approval was based on thirteen published articles concerning clinical trials sponsored by Medtronic; each article, however, was by a physician who had a financial interest in INFUSE. Following FDA approval, patients treated with INFUSE began incurring

---

[2] Page 675 in Concise edition.

serious health problems. Soon the national press reported the dire health issues surround use of INFUSE as well as that the physicians authoring the articles leading to FDA approval stood to benefit and did benefit from INFUSE's approval. Congressional hearings ensued, Medtronic share price fell, and a securities class action based on misrepresentations in the published articles was filed. The suit alleged that Medtronic had engaged in a *scheme* to defraud. The district court's granted Medtronic's summary judgment on the ground that it did not meet the *Janus* test as a primary participant in the misrepresentations linked to the published articles. The Eighth Circuit reversed.]

The broader scope of scheme liability under Rule 10b–5(a) and (c) potentially offers plaintiffs a means to circumvent *Janus*—a situation we encountered in *Public Pension Fund Group v. KV Pharmaceutical Co.*, 679 F.3d 972 (8th Cir. 2012). In that case, investors asserted false statement claims against a pharmaceutical company for misrepresenting its compliance with FDA regulations in its SEC filings. The investors also attempted to assert a scheme liability claim against two of the pharmaceutical company's officers, alleging only that the officers had knowledge of the company's misrepresentations. We rejected the scheme liability claim, emphasizing that "a scheme liability claim must be based on conduct beyond misrepresentations or omissions actionable under Rule 10b–5(b)." *Id.* at 987. Otherwise, plaintiffs could simply recast false statement claims barred under *Janus* as scheme liability claims. *See id.* Without alleging that the officers engaged in conduct beyond misrepresentations, allegations that the officers simply knew about the company's misrepresentations were insufficient to support a scheme liability claim. *Id.* Accordingly, a plaintiff cannot support a scheme liability claim by simply repackaging a fraudulent misrepresentation as a scheme to defraud. Rather, a plaintiff must allege some deceptive act other than the fraudulent misrepresentation. . . .

Here, Appellants allege conduct beyond mere misrepresentations or omissions actionable under Rule 10b–5(b). Appellants' scheme liability claim alleges that Medtronic shaped the content of medical journals by "pa[ying] physicians . . . to induce their complicity in concealing adverse events and side effects associated with the use of INFUSE and overstating the disadvantages of alternative bone graft procedures." Although the scheme liability claim also includes allegations that Medtronic edited language in the clinical studies that the physicians ultimately published, the act of paying physicians to induce their complicity is the allegation at the heart of the scheme liability claim. Paying someone else to make a misrepresentation is not itself a misrepresentation. Thus, Appellants do not merely repackage allegations of misrepresentation as allegations of a scheme. *Janus* and *KV Pharmaceuticals* require some conduct other than a misrepresentation to support a scheme liability claim. They do not hold that the alleged scheme can never involve any misrepresentation in order for the scheme liability claim to survive. *See, e.g., In re Smith Barney*, 884 F. Supp. 2d at 161 (sustaining scheme liability claim where alleged conduct included but was not limited to misleadingly disclosing fees). Accordingly, because Medtronic's alleged deceptive conduct goes beyond mere misrepresentations or omissions, *Janus* does not bar Appellants' scheme liability claim.

The second part of Medtronic's argument concerns whether Appellants have sufficiently pleaded that the market relied on Medtronic's conduct as a matter of law. In *Stoneridge*, Charter Communications and its suppliers engaged in sham transactions designed to enable Charter to falsify its financial statements. 552 U.S. at 152–55. Investors sued the suppliers, asserting both a false statement claim and a scheme liability claim. While the investors argued that the suppliers' participation in the sham transactions enabled Charter to falsify its statements, the Supreme Court held that the investors could not demonstrate that they relied on the suppliers' conduct. *Id.* at 159. "Reliance by the plaintiff upon the defendant's deceptive acts is an essential element of the § 10(b) private cause of action. It ensures that, for liability to arise, the 'requisite causal connection between a defendant's misrepresentation and a plaintiff's injury' exists as a predicate for liability." *Id.* (quoting *Basic Inc. v. Levinson*, 485 U.S. 224, 243, 108 S. Ct. 978, 99 L. Ed. 2d 194 (1988)). The Court rejected the false statements claim, concluding that the causal connection between the suppliers and the falsified financial statements was too attenuated to support a finding of market reliance where the suppliers' conduct did not satisfy any presumption of reliance and the investing public did not have knowledge of the suppliers' deceptive acts. *Id.* . . .

Unlike the conduct at issue in *Stoneridge*, the causal connection between Medtronic's alleged deceptive conduct and the information on which the market relied is not too remote to support a finding of reliance. Medtronic's alleged deceptive conduct consists of manipulating the clinical trials by paying the physician-authors to conceal adverse effects and to overstate the disadvantages of alternative procedures. Appellants alleged in their complaint that investors directly relied on the resulting favorable clinical trials. Indeed, according to the Appellants' amended complaint, in speaking with potential investors, Medtronic's CEO specifically emphasized that the company's products' strong clinical trial performance undergirded Medtronic's competitiveness and sustainability. As a result, taking the allegations as true, Medtronic's deceptive conduct directly caused the production of the information on which the market relied. Unlike the suppliers' conduct in *Stoneridge*, Medtronic's purported conduct would not merely assist or enable the physician-authors to deceive the market. Rather, Medtronic's alleged conduct would deceive the market with the assistance of the physician-authors. A company cannot instruct individuals to take a certain action, pay to induce them to do it, and then claim any causal connection is too remote when they follow through. In this way, Medtronic's alleged manipulative conduct directly caused the biased clinical trial results that the market relied upon. This alleged causal connection is sufficient to support a finding of reliance. . . .

III.

For the reasons discussed above, we vacate summary judgment and remand for proceedings not inconsistent with this opinion.

6. CAUSAL RELATIONSHIP

Page 896.[3] Substitute the following for *Basic Inc. v. Levinson*:

Halliburton Co. v. Erica P. John Fund, Inc.

Supreme Court of the United States, 2014.
___ U.S. ___, 134 S.Ct. 2398, 189 L.Ed.2d 339.

■ ROBERTS, C. J.

I

Respondent Erica P. John Fund, Inc. (EPJ Fund), is the lead plaintiff in a putative class action against Halliburton and one of its executives (collectively Halliburton) alleging violations of *section 10(b)* of the Securities Exchange Act of 1934 . . . and Securities and Exchange Commission *Rule 10b–5* . . . . According to EPJ Fund, between June 3, 1999, and December 7, 2001, Halliburton made a series of misrepresentations regarding its potential liability in asbestos litigation, its expected revenue from certain construction contracts, and the anticipated benefits of its merger with another company—all in an attempt to inflate the price of its stock. Halliburton subsequently made a number of corrective disclosures, which, EPJ Fund contends, caused the company's stock price to drop and investors to lose money. . . .

II

Halliburton urges us to overrule . . . presumption of reliance [of *Basic Inc. v. Levinson*, 485 U.S. 224 (1988)] and to instead require every securities fraud plaintiff to prove that he actually relied on the defendant's misrepresentation in deciding to buy or sell a company's stock. . . .

A

The reliance element " 'ensures that there is a proper connection between a defendant's misrepresentation and a plaintiff's injury.' " 568 U.S., at ___ . . . (quoting *Halliburton I*, 563 U.S., at ___ . . . . "The traditional (and most direct) way a plaintiff can demonstrate reliance is by showing that he was aware of a company's statement and engaged in

---

[3]   Page 679 of Concise edition.

a relevant transaction—*e.g.,* purchasing common stock—based on that specific misrepresentation." *Id.,* at ___ (slip op., at 4).

In *Basic,* however, we recognized that requiring such direct proof of reliance "would place an unnecessarily unrealistic evidentiary burden on the *Rule 10b–5* plaintiff who has traded on an impersonal market." 485 U.S., at 245. That is because, even assuming an investor could prove that he was aware of the misrepresentation, he would still have to "show a speculative state of facts, *i.e.,* how he would have acted . . . if the misrepresentation had not been made." *Ibid.*

We also noted that "[r]equiring proof of individualized reliance" from every securities fraud plaintiff "effectively would . . . prevent[ ][plaintiffs] from proceeding with a class action" in *Rule 10b–5* suits. If every plaintiff had to prove direct reliance on the defendant's misrepresentation, "individual issues then would . . . overwhelm[ ] the common ones," making certification under *Rule 23(b)(3)* inappropriate.

To address these concerns, *Basic* held that securities fraud plaintiffs can in certain circumstances satisfy the reliance element of a *Rule 10b–5* action by invoking a rebuttable presumption of reliance, rather than proving direct reliance on a misrepresentation. The Court based that presumption on what is known as the "fraud-on-the-market" theory, which holds that "the market price of shares traded on well-developed markets reflects all publicly available information, and, hence, any material misrepresentations." *Id.,* at 246. The Court also noted that, rather than scrutinize every piece of public information about a company for himself, the typical "investor who buys or sells stock at the price set by the market does so in reliance on the integrity of that price"—the belief that it reflects all public, material information. *Id.,* at 247. As a result, whenever the investor buys or sells stock at the market price, his "reliance on any public material misrepresentations . . . may be presumed for purposes of a *Rule 10b–5* action." *Ibid.* . . .

At the same time, *Basic* emphasized that the presumption of reliance was rebuttable rather than conclusive. Specifically, "[a]ny showing that severs the link between the alleged misrepresentation and either the price received (or paid) by the plaintiff, or his decision to trade at a fair market price, will be sufficient to rebut the presumption of reliance." 485 U.S., at 248. So for example, if a defendant could show that the alleged misrepresentation did not, for whatever reason, actually affect the market price, or that a plaintiff would have bought or sold the stock even had he been aware that the stock's price was tainted by fraud, then the presumption of reliance would not apply. *Id.,* at 248–249. In either of those cases, a plaintiff would have to prove that he directly relied on the defendant's misrepresentation in buying or selling the stock.

B

. . .

2

Halliburton's primary argument for overruling *Basic* is that the decision rested on two premises that can no longer withstand scrutiny. The first premise concerns what is known as the "efficient capital markets hypothesis." *Basic* stated that "the market price of shares traded on well-developed markets reflects all publicly available information, and, hence, any material misrepresentations." *Id.,* at 246. From that statement, Halliburton concludes that the *Basic* Court espoused "a robust view of market efficiency" that is no longer tenable, for " 'overwhelming empirical evidence' now 'suggests that capital markets are not fundamentally efficient.' " Brief for Petitioners 14–16 (quoting Lev & de Villiers, Stock Price Crashes and 10b–5 Damages: A Legal, Economic, and Policy Analysis, *47 Stan. L. Rev 7, 20 (1994)*). To support this contention, Halliburton cites studies purporting to show that "public information is often not incorporated immediately (much less rationally) into market prices." . . .

Halliburton does not, of course, maintain that capital markets are *always* inefficient. Rather, in its view, *Basic*'s fundamental error was to ignore the fact that " 'efficiency is not a binary, yes or no question.' " . . . The markets for some securities are more efficient than the markets for others, and even a single market can process different kinds of information more or less efficiently, depending on how widely the information is disseminated and how easily it is understood. . . . Yet *Basic*, Halliburton asserts, glossed over these nuances, assuming a false dichotomy that renders the presumption of reliance both underinclusive and overinclusive: A misrepresentation can distort a stock's market price even in a generally inefficient market, and a misrepresentation can leave a stock's market price unaffected even in a generally efficient one. . . .

Halliburton's criticisms fail to take *Basic* on its own terms. Halliburton focuses on the debate among economists about the degree to which the market price of a company's stock reflects public information about the company—and thus the degree to which an investor can earn an abnormal, above-market return by trading on such information. . . . That debate is not new. Indeed, the *Basic* Court acknowledged it and declined to enter the fray, declaring that "[w]e need not determine by adjudication what economists and social scientists have debated through the use of sophisticated statistical analysis and the application of economic theory." 485 U.S., at 246–247, n. 24. To recognize the presumption of reliance, the Court explained, was not "conclusively to adopt any particular theory of how quickly and completely publicly available information is reflected in market price." *Id.,* at 248, n. 28. The Court instead based the presumption on the fairly modest premise that "market professionals generally consider most publicly announced material statements about companies, thereby affecting stock market prices." *Id.,* at 247, n. 24. *Basic*'s presumption of reliance thus does not rest on a "binary" view of market efficiency. Indeed, in making the presumption rebuttable, *Basic* recognized that market efficiency is a matter of degree and accordingly made it a matter of proof.

The academic debates discussed by Halliburton have not refuted the modest premise underlying the presumption of reliance. Even the foremost critics of the efficient-capital-markets hypothesis acknowledge that public information generally affects stock prices. See, *e.g.,* Shiller, We'll Share the Honors, and Agree to Disagree, N. Y. Times, Oct. 27, 2013, p. BU6 ("Of course, prices reflect available information"). . . . Debates about the precise *degree* to which stock prices accurately reflect public information are thus largely beside the point. "That the . . . price [of a stock] may be inaccurate does not detract from the fact that false statements affect it, and cause loss," which is "all that *Basic* requires." *Schleicher v. Wendt,* 618 F.3d 679, 685 (CA7 2010)(Easterbrook, C. J.). . . . Halliburton has not identified the kind of fundamental shift in economic theory that could justify overruling a precedent on the ground that it misunderstood, or has since been overtaken by, economic realities. . . .

Halliburton also contests a second premise underlying the *Basic* presumption: the notion that investors "invest 'in reliance on the integrity of [the market] price.' " . . . Halliburton identifies a number of classes of investors for whom "price integrity" is supposedly "marginal or irrelevant." . . . The primary example is the value investor, who believes that certain stocks are undervalued or overvalued and attempts to "beat the market" by buying the undervalued stocks and selling the overvalued ones. . . . See also Brief for Vivendi S. A. as *Amicus Curiae* 3–10 (describing the investment strategies of day traders, volatility arbitragers, and value investors). If many investors "are indifferent to prices," Halliburton contends, then courts should not presume that investors rely on the integrity of those prices and any misrepresentations incorporated into them. . . .

But *Basic* never denied the existence of such investors. As we recently explained, *Basic* concluded only that "it is reasonable to presume that *most* investors—knowing that they have little hope of outperforming the market in the long run based solely on their analysis of publicly available information—will rely on the security's market price as an unbiased assessment of the security's value in light of all public information." *Amgen,* 568 U.S., at ___ . . . (emphasis added).

In any event, there is no reason to suppose that even Halliburton's main counterexample—the value investor—is as indifferent to the integrity of market prices as Halliburton suggests. Such an investor implicitly relies on the fact that a stock's market price will eventually reflect material information—how else could the market correction on which his profit depends occur? To be sure, the value investor "does not believe that the market price accurately reflects public information *at the time he transacts.*" *Post*, at 11. But to indirectly rely on a misstatement in the sense relevant for the *Basic* presumption, he need only trade stock based on the belief that the market price will incorporate public information within a reasonable period. The value investor also presumably tries to estimate *how* undervalued or overvalued a particular stock is, and such estimates can be skewed by a market price tainted by fraud. . . .

C . . .

Finally, Halliburton and its *amici* contend that, by facilitating securities class actions, the *Basic* presumption produces a number of serious and harmful consequences. Such class actions, they say, allow plaintiffs to extort large settlements from defendants for meritless claims; punish innocent shareholders, who end up having to pay settlements and judgments; impose excessive costs on businesses; and consume a disproportionately large share of judicial resources. . . .

These concerns are more appropriately addressed to Congress, which has in fact responded, to some extent, to many of the issues raised by Halliburton and its *amici*. Congress has, for example, enacted the Private Securities Litigation Reform Act of 1995 (PSLRA), 109 Stat. 737, which sought to combat perceived abuses in securities litigation . . . . And to prevent plaintiffs from circumventing these restrictions by bringing securities class actions under state law in state court, Congress also enacted the Securities Litigation Uniform Standards Act of 1998, 112 Stat. 3227, which precludes many state law class actions alleging securities fraud. Such legislation demonstrates Congress's willingness to consider policy concerns of the sort that Halliburton says should lead us to overrule *Basic*.

III

Halliburton proposes two alternatives to overruling *Basic* that would alleviate what it regards as the decision's most serious flaws. The first alternative would require plaintiffs to prove that a defendant's misrepresentation actually affected the stock price—so-called "price impact"—in order to invoke the *Basic* presumption. . . . Halliburton's second proposed alternative would allow defendants to rebut the presumption of reliance with evidence of a *lack* of price impact, not only at the merits stage—which all agree defendants may already do—but also before class certification.

A

 . . . [T]o invoke the *Basic* presumption, a plaintiff must prove that: (1) the alleged misrepresentations were publicly known, (2) they were material, (3) the stock traded in an efficient market, and (4) the plaintiff traded the stock between when the misrepresentations were made and when the truth was revealed. . . . The first three prerequisites are directed at price impact—"whether the alleged misrepresentations affected the market price in the first place." *Halliburton I*, 563 U.S., at

___ (slip op., at 8). In the absence of price impact, *Basic*'s fraud-on-the-market theory and presumption of reliance collapse. . . . Halliburton argues that since the *Basic* presumption hinges on price impact, plaintiffs should be required to prove it directly in order to invoke the presumption. Proving the presumption's prerequisites, which are at best an imperfect proxy for price impact, should not suffice.

Far from a modest refinement of the *Basic* presumption, this proposal would radically alter the required showing for the reliance element of the *Rule 10b–5* cause of action. What is called the *Basic* presumption actually incorporates two constituent presumptions: First, if a plaintiff shows that the defendant's misrepresentation was public and material and that the stock traded in a generally efficient market, he is entitled to a presumption that the misrepresentation affected the stock price. Second, if the plaintiff also shows that he purchased the stock at the market price during the relevant period, he is entitled to a further presumption that he purchased the stock in reliance on the defendant's misrepresentation.

By requiring plaintiffs to prove price impact directly, Halliburton's proposal would take away the first constituent presumption. Halliburton's argument for doing so is the same as its primary argument for overruling the *Basic* presumption altogether: Because market efficiency is not a yes-or-no proposition, a public, material misrepresentation might not affect a stock's price even in a generally efficient market. But as explained, *Basic* never suggested otherwise; that is why it affords defendants an opportunity to rebut the presumption by showing, among other things, that the particular misrepresentation at issue did not affect the stock's market price. For the same reasons we declined to completely jettison the *Basic* presumption, we decline to effectively jettison half of it by revising the prerequisites for invoking it.

B

Even if plaintiffs need not directly prove price impact to invoke the *Basic* presumption, Halliburton contends that defendants should at least be allowed to defeat the presumption at the class certification stage through evidence that the misrepresentation did not in fact affect the stock price. We agree.

1

There is no dispute that defendants may introduce such evidence at the merits stage to rebut the *Basic* presumption. *Basic* itself "made clear that the presumption was just that, and could be rebutted by appropriate evidence," including evidence that the asserted misrepresentation (or its correction) did not affect the market price of the defendant's stock. . . . Nor is there any dispute that defendants may introduce price impact evidence at the class certification stage, so long as it is for the purpose of countering a plaintiff's showing of market efficiency, rather than directly rebutting the presumption. . . .

After all, plaintiffs themselves can and do introduce evidence of the *existence* of price impact in connection with "event studies"—regression analyses that seek to show that the market price of the defendant's stock tends to respond to pertinent publicly reported events. See Brief for Law Professors as *Amici Curiae* 25–28. In this case, for example, EPJ Fund submitted an event study of various episodes that might have been expected to affect the price of Halliburton's stock, in order to demonstrate that the market for that stock takes account of material, public information about the company. See App. 217–230 (describing the results of the study). The episodes examined by EPJ Fund's event study included one of the alleged misrepresentations that form the basis of the Fund's suit. . . .

Defendants—like plaintiffs—may accordingly submit price impact evidence prior to class certification. . . .

Suppose a defendant at the certification stage submits an event study looking at the impact on the price of its stock from six discrete events, in an effort to refute the plaintiffs' claim of general market efficiency. All agree the defendant may do this. Suppose one of the six events is the specific misrepresentation asserted by the plaintiffs. All agree that this too is perfectly acceptable. Now suppose the district court determines that, despite the defendant's study, the plaintiff has carried its burden to prove market efficiency, but that the evidence shows no price impact with respect to the specific misrepresentation challenged in the suit. The evidence at the certification stage thus shows an efficient market, on which the alleged misrepresentation had no price impact. . . . [U]nder EPJ Fund's view, the plaintiffs' action should be certified and proceed as a class action (with all that entails), even though the fraud-on-the-market theory does not apply and common reliance thus cannot be presumed.

Such a result is inconsistent with *Basic*'s own logic. Under *Basic*'s fraud-on-the-market theory, market efficiency and the other prerequisites for invoking the presumption constitute an indirect way of showing price impact. As explained, it is appropriate to allow plaintiffs to rely on this indirect proxy for price impact, rather than requiring them to prove price impact directly, given *Basic*'s rationales for recognizing a presumption of reliance in the first place. . . .

But an indirect proxy should not preclude direct evidence when such evidence is available. As we explained in *Basic*, "[a]ny showing that severs the link between the alleged misrepresentation and . . . the price received (or paid) by the plaintiff . . . will be sufficient to rebut the presumption of reliance" because "the basis for finding that the fraud had been transmitted through market price would be gone." 485 U.S., at 248. And without the presumption of reliance, a *Rule 10b–5* suit cannot proceed as a class action: Each plaintiff would have to prove reliance individually, so common issues would not "predominate" over individual ones, as required by *Rule 23(b)(3)*. *Id., at 242.* Price impact is thus an essential precondition for any *Rule 10b–5* class action. While *Basic* allows plaintiffs to establish that precondition indirectly, it does not require courts to ignore a defendant's direct, more salient evidence showing that the alleged misrepresentation did not actually affect the stock's market price and, consequently, that the *Basic* presumption does not apply. . . .

Our choice in this case, then, is not between allowing price impact evidence at the class certification stage or relegating it to the merits. Evidence of price impact will be before the court at the certification stage in any event. The choice, rather, is between limiting the price impact inquiry before class certification to indirect evidence, or allowing consideration of direct evidence as well. As explained, we see no reason to artificially limit the inquiry at the certification stage to indirect evidence of price impact. Defendants may seek to defeat the *Basic* presumption at that stage through direct as well as indirect price impact evidence.

More than 25 years ago, we held that plaintiffs could satisfy the reliance element of the *Rule 10b–5* cause of action by invoking a presumption that a public, material misrepresentation will distort the price of stock traded in an efficient market, and that anyone who purchases the stock at the market price may be considered to have done so in reliance on the misrepresentation. We adhere to that decision and decline to modify the prerequisites for invoking the presumption of reliance. But to maintain the consistency of the presumption with the class certification requirements of *Federal Rule of Civil Procedure 23*, defendants must be afforded an opportunity before class certification to defeat the presumption through evidence that an alleged misrepresentation did not actually affect the market price of the stock.

Because the courts below denied Halliburton that opportunity, we vacate the judgment of the Court of Appeals for the Fifth Circuit and remand the case for further proceedings consistent with this opinion.

It is so ordered.

■ JUSTICE GINSBURG, with whom JUSTICE BREYER and JUSTICE SOTOMAYOR join, concurring.

Advancing price impact consideration from the merits stage to the certification stage may broaden the scope of discovery available at certification. . . . But the Court recognizes that it is incumbent upon the defendant to show the absence of price impact. . . . The Court's judgment, therefore, should impose no heavy toll on securities-fraud plaintiffs with tenable claims. On that understanding, I join the Court's opinion.

■ JUSTICE THOMAS, with whom JUSTICE SCALIA and JUSTICE ALITO join, concurring in the judgment.

* * *

In *GAMCO Investors v. Vivendi Universal*, 838 F.3d 214 (2d Cir. 2016), plaintiffs had opted out of a class action against Vivendi and pursued their individual claims alleging that during the time of their purchases Vivendi had engaged in a series of misrepresentations that concealed various "liquidity" problems the firm was having and such concealment had the effect of inflating shares' market price above what the price would have been had the various liquidity issues not be concealed. Plaintiffs were so-called "value investors" who purchased their shares in the belief that the market price of Vivendi shares were less than value the plaintiffs believed the shares were worth. The district court dismissal of the case was affirmed by the Second Circuit on the basis that evidence produced by the defendant established that the plaintiff's valuation model did not focus on such liquidity concerns so that the plaintiffs would have purchased Vivendi shares even if the liquidity issues had been disclose. The plaintiffs' case was not assisted by the fact that even after they became aware of the fraud they continued to purchase Vivendi shares.

The inquiry into the price impact of an alleged misrepresentation in fraud on the market cases frequently occurs in the context of an event study, a statistical method for determining whether some corporate event, e.g., the announce of earnings, is associated with a statistically significant change in the price of a company's stock. The main inputs for any event study are benchmark returns provided by a broad index such as the S&P Industrial 500, the historical stock return of the company or companies being observed, and standard statistical methods to measure statistical significance. As originally developed by financial economists, event studies observed phenomenon shared by a portfolio of companies, e.g., they each announced an earnings increase. Event studies in securities litigation, however, almost always involve only a single-firm as they seek to isolate and measure price moves of a particular (defendant) firm involved in the litigation. Importing a methodology long-used by economists for studies of phenomena shared by multiple firms into a single-firm context raises profound methodological concerns, namely in terms of the model's predictive power. *See e.g.,* J. B. Heaton & Alon Brav, Event Studies in Securities Litigation: Low Power, Confounding Effects, and Bias, 93 Wash. U. L. Rev. 583 (2015). This concern is beginning to be reflected in court decisions. *In re Petrobras Securities Litig.,* 862 F.3d 250 (2nd Cir. 2017), held the defendants could not use an event study to establish—without consideration of other evidence—that alleged securities fraud had no impact on a stock price of the defendant company. Judge Garaufis in his decision notes that "event studies offer the seductive promise of hard numbers and dispassionate truth, but methodological constraints limit their utility in the context of single-firm analyses. *Id.* at 278. Recall that the fifth *Cammer* factor for determining whether a particular security trades in an efficient market is the security's responsiveness to new information. *Waggoner v. Barclays PLC,* 875 F.3d 79 (2nd Cir. 2017), held that when the weight of other factors support a finding a particular security traded in an efficient market there is no need to consider the absence of price impact from an event study.

CHAPTER 13

INSIDER TRADING

2. THE FEDERAL DISCLOSE OR ABSTAIN REQUIREMENT

Page 979.[1] Insert the following after *Dirks v. Securities and Exchange Commission*:

Salman v. United States

Supreme Court of the United States, 2016.
___ U.S. ___, 137 S.Ct. 420, 196 L.Ed.2d 351.

■ JUSTICE ALITO delivered the opinion of the Court.

Section 10(b) of the Securities Exchange Act of 1934 and the Securities and Exchange Commission's Rule 10b–5 prohibit undisclosed trading on inside corporate information by individuals who are under a duty of trust and confidence that prohibits them from secretly using such information for their personal advantage. . . . Individuals under this duty may face criminal and civil liability for trading on inside information (unless they make appropriate disclosures ahead of time).

These persons also may not tip inside information to others for trading. The tippee acquires the tipper's duty to disclose or abstain from trading if the tippee knows the information was disclosed in breach of the tipper's duty, and the tippee may commit securities fraud by trading in disregard of that knowledge. In *Dirks* v. *SEC*, 463 U.S. 646 . . . , this Court explained that a tippee's liability for trading on inside information hinges on whether the tipper breached a fiduciary duty by disclosing the information. A tipper breaches such a fiduciary duty, we held, when the tipper discloses the inside information for a personal benefit. And, we went on to say, a jury can infer a personal benefit—and thus a breach of the tipper's duty—where the tipper receives something of value in exchange for the tip or "makes a gift of confidential information to a trading relative or friend." *Id.*, at 664. . . .

I

Maher Kara was an investment banker in Citigroup's healthcare investment banking group. He dealt with highly confidential information about mergers and acquisitions involving Citigroup's clients. Maher enjoyed a close relationship with his older brother, Mounir Kara (known as Michael). After Maher started at Citigroup, he began discussing aspects of his job with Michael. At first he relied on Michael's chemistry background to help him grasp scientific concepts relevant to his new job. Then, while their father was battling cancer, the brothers discussed

---

[1] Page 745 of Concise edition at end of *Dirks*.

companies that dealt with innovative cancer treatment and pain management techniques. Michael began to trade on the information Maher shared with him. At first, Maher was unaware of his brother's trading activity, but eventually he began to suspect that it was taking place.

Ultimately, Maher began to assist Michael's trading by sharing inside information with his brother about pending mergers and acquisitions. Maher sometimes used code words to communicate corporate information to his brother. Other times, he shared inside information about deals he was not working on in order to avoid detection. . . . Without his younger brother's knowledge, Michael fed the information to others—including [Bassam] Salman, Michael's friend and Maher's brother-in-law. By the time the authorities caught on, Salman had made over $1.5 million in profits that he split with another relative who executed trades via a brokerage account on Salman's behalf.

Salman was indicted on one count of conspiracy to commit securities fraud, see 18 U.S.C. § 371, and four counts of securities fraud, see 15 U.S.C. §§ 78j(b) . . . [and] 17 CFR § 240.10b–5. Facing charges of their own, both Maher and Michael pleaded guilty and testified at Salman's trial.

The evidence at trial established that Maher and Michael enjoyed a "very close relationship." . . . Maher testified that he shared inside information with his brother to benefit him and with the expectation that his brother would trade on it. While Maher explained that he disclosed the information in large part to appease Michael (who pestered him incessantly for it), he also testified that he tipped his brother to "help him" and to "fulfil[l] whatever needs he had." . . . For instance, Michael once called Maher and told him that "he needed a favor." . . . Maher offered his brother money but Michael asked for information instead. Maher then disclosed an upcoming acquisition. *Ibid.* Although he instantly regretted the tip and called his brother back to implore him not to trade, Maher expected his brother to do so anyway. . . .

Michael testified that he became friends with Salman when Maher was courting Salman's sister and later began sharing Maher's tips with Salman. As he explained at trial, "any time a major deal came in, [Salman] was the first on my phone list." *Id.*, at 258. Michael also testified that he told Salman that the information was coming from Maher. . . .

After a jury trial in the Northern District of California, Salman was convicted on all counts. He was sentenced to 36 months of imprisonment, three years of supervised release, and over $730,000 in restitution. . . . Salman appealed to the Ninth Circuit. While his appeal was pending, the Second Circuit issued its opinion in *United States* v. *Newman*, 773 F.3d 438 (2014), cert. denied, 577 U.S. ___, 136 S. Ct. 242, 193 L. Ed. 2d 133 (2015). There, the Second Circuit reversed the convictions of two portfolio managers who traded on inside information. The *Newman* defendants were "several steps removed from the corporate insiders" and the court found that "there was no evidence that either was aware of the source of the inside information." 773 F.3d, at 443. The court acknowledged that *Dirks* and Second Circuit case law allow a factfinder to infer a personal benefit to the tipper from a gift of confidential information to a trading relative or friend. 773 F.3d, at 452. But the court concluded that, "[t]o the extent" *Dirks* permits "such an inference," the inference "is impermissible in the absence of proof of a meaningfully close personal relationship that generates an exchange that is objective, consequential, and represents at least a potential gain of a pecuniary or similarly valuable nature." 773 F.3d, at 452.[1]

Pointing to *Newman*, Salman argued that his conviction should be reversed. While the evidence established that Maher made a gift of trading information to Michael and that Salman knew it, there was no evidence that Maher received anything of "a pecuniary or similarly valuable nature" in exchange—or that Salman knew of any such benefit. The Ninth Circuit disagreed and affirmed Salman's conviction. 792 F.3d 1087. The court reasoned that the case was governed by *Dirks's* holding that a tipper benefits personally by making a gift of confidential information to a trading relative or friend. . . .

We granted certiorari to resolve the tension between the Second Circuit's *Newman* decision and the Ninth Circuit's decision in this case.[2]
. . .

II

A

In this case, Salman contends that an insider's "gift of confidential information to a trading relative or friend," *Dirks*, 463 U.S., at 664, 103 S. Ct. 3255, 77 L. Ed. 2d 911, is not enough to establish securities fraud. Instead, Salman argues, a tipper does not personally benefit unless the tipper's goal in disclosing inside information is to obtain money, property, or something of tangible value. . . . Salman contends that gift situations

---

[1]   The Second Circuit also reversed the *Newman* defendants' convictions because the Government introduced no evidence that the defendants knew the information they traded on came from insiders or that the insiders received a personal benefit in exchange for the tips. 773 F.3d, at 453–454. This case does not implicate those issues.

[2]   *Dirks* v. *SEC*, 463 U.S. 646, 103 S. Ct. 3255, 77 L. Ed. 2d 911 (1983), established the personal-benefit framework in a case brought under the classical theory of insider-trading liability, which applies "when a corporate insider" or his tippee "trades in the securities of [the tipper's] corporation on the basis of material, nonpublic information." *United States* v. *O'Hagan*, 521 U.S. 642, 651–652, 117 S. Ct. 2199, 138 L. Ed. 2d 724 (1997). In such a case, the defendant breaches a duty to, and takes advantage of, the shareholders of his corporation. By contrast, the misappropriation theory holds that a person commits securities fraud "when he misappropriates confidential information for securities trading purposes, in breach of a duty owed to the source of the information" such as an employer or client. *Id.*, at 652, 117 S. Ct. 2199, 138 L. Ed. 2d 724. In such a case, the defendant breaches a duty to, and defrauds, the source of the information, as opposed to the shareholders of his corporation. The Court of Appeals observed that this is a misappropriation case, 792 F.3d, 1087, 1092, n. 4 (CA9 2015), while the Government represents that both theories apply on the facts of this case, Brief for United States 15, n. 1. We need not resolve the question. The parties do not dispute that *Dirks's* personal-benefit analysis applies in both classical and misappropriation cases, so we will proceed on the assumption that it does.

create especially troubling problems for remote tippees—that is, tippees who receive inside information from another tippee, rather than the tipper—who may have no knowledge of the relationship between the original tipper and tippee and thus may not know why the tipper made the disclosure. . . .

The Government disagrees and argues that a gift of confidential information to anyone, not just a "trading relative or friend," is enough to prove securities fraud. . . . Under the Government's view, a tipper personally benefits whenever the tipper discloses confidential trading information for a noncorporate purpose. Accordingly, a gift to a friend, a family member, or anyone else would support the inference that the tipper exploited the trading value of inside information for personal purposes and thus personally benefited from the disclosure. . . .

The Government also argues that Salman's concerns about unlimited and indeterminate liability for remote tippees are significantly alleviated by other statutory elements that prosecutors must satisfy to convict a tippee for insider trading. The Government observes that, in order to establish a defendant's criminal liability as a tippee, it must prove beyond a reasonable doubt that the tipper expected that the information being disclosed would be used in securities trading. . . . The Government also notes that, to establish a defendant's criminal liability as a tippee, it must prove that the tippee knew that the tipper breached a duty—in other words, that the tippee knew that the tipper disclosed the information for a personal benefit and that the tipper expected trading to ensue. . . .

B

We adhere to *Dirks,* which easily resolves the narrow issue presented here.

In *Dirks,* we explained that a tippee is exposed to liability for trading on inside information only if the tippee participates in a breach of the tipper's fiduciary duty. Whether the tipper breached that duty depends "in large part on the purpose of the disclosure" to the tippee. 463 U.S., at 662 . . . . "[T]he test," we explained, "is whether the insider personally will benefit, directly or indirectly, from his disclosure." *Ibid.* Thus, the disclosure of confidential information without personal benefit is not enough. In determining whether a tipper derived a personal benefit, we instructed courts to "focus on objective criteria, *i.e.,* whether the insider receives a direct or indirect personal benefit from the disclosure, such as a pecuniary gain or a reputational benefit that will translate into future earnings." *Id.,* at 663 . . . . This personal benefit can "often" be inferred "from objective facts and circumstances," we explained, such as "a relationship between the insider and the recipient that suggests a *quid pro quo* from the latter, or an intention to benefit the particular recipient." *Id.,* at 664 . . . . In particular, we held that "[t]he elements of fiduciary duty and exploitation of nonpublic information also exist *when an insider makes a gift of confidential information to a trading relative or friend." Ibid.* (emphasis added). In such cases, "[t]he tip and trade resemble trading by the insider followed by a gift of the profits to the recipient." *Ibid.* We then applied this gift-giving principle to resolve *Dirks* itself, finding it dispositive that the tippers "received no monetary or personal benefit" from their tips to Dirks, "*nor was their purpose to make a gift of valuable information to Dirks.*" *Id.,* at 667 . . . (emphasis added).

Our discussion of gift giving resolves this case. Maher, the tipper, provided inside information to a close relative, his brother Michael. *Dirks* makes clear that a tipper breaches a fiduciary duty by making a gift of confidential information to "a trading relative," and that rule is sufficient to resolve the case at hand. As Salman's counsel acknowledged at oral argument, Maher would have breached his duty had he personally traded on the information here himself then given the proceeds as a gift to his brother. Tr. of Oral Arg. 3–4. It is obvious that Maher would personally benefit in that situation. But Maher effectively achieved the same result by disclosing the information to Michael, and allowing him to trade on it. *Dirks* appropriately prohibits that approach, as well. . . . *Dirks* specifies that when a tipper gives inside information to "a trading relative or friend," the jury can infer that the tipper meant to provide the equivalent of a cash gift. In such situations, the tipper benefits personally because giving a gift of trading information is the same thing as trading by the tipper followed by a gift of the proceeds. Here, by disclosing confidential information as a gift to his brother with the expectation that he would trade on it, Maher breached his duty of trust and confidence to Citigroup and its clients—a duty Salman acquired, and breached himself, by trading on the information with full knowledge that it had been improperly disclosed.

To the extent the Second Circuit held that the tipper must also receive something of a "pecuniary or similarly valuable nature" in exchange for a gift to family or friends, *Newman,* 773 F.3d, at 452, we agree with the Ninth Circuit that this requirement is inconsistent with *Dirks.*

C

Salman points out that many insider-trading cases—including several that *Dirks* cited—involved insiders who personally profited through the misuse of trading information. But this observation does not undermine the test *Dirks* articulated and applied. . . . Making a gift of inside information to a relative like Michael is little different from trading on the information, obtaining the profits, and doling them out to the trading relative. The tipper benefits either way. The facts of this case illustrate the point: In one of their tipper-tippee interactions, Michael asked Maher for a favor, declined Maher's offer of money, and instead requested and received lucrative trading information.

. . .

III

Salman's jury was properly instructed that a personal benefit includes "the benefit one would obtain from simply making a gift of confidential information to a trading relative." . . . As the Court of Appeals noted, "the Government presented direct evidence that the disclosure was intended as a gift of market-sensitive information." 792 F.3d, at 1094. And, as Salman conceded below, this evidence is sufficient to sustain his conviction under our reading of *Dirks*. . . . Accordingly, the Ninth Circuit's judgment is affirmed.

It is so ordered.

CHAPTER 14

SHAREHOLDER SUITS

1. INTRODUCTION

Page 1021.[1] Insert the following before the last paragraph of the Note on the Empirical Studies of Shareholder Litigation:

The contemporary concern for shareholder litigation is the near epidemic scale of shareholder suits alleging officer and director breaches of duties in connection with mergers and acquisitions. For example, a study of 2012 reported that 92 percent of acquisitions in excess of $100 million attracted at least one fiduciary class action. Robert M. Daines & Olga Koumrian, Cornerstone Research, Shareholder Litigation Involving Mergers and Acquisitions 1 (Feb. 2013). Such class action suits are customarily brought on behalf of the shareholders of the acquired firm and allege a range of misconduct, such as their board failing to obtain a better price, there being disclosure breaches in seeking stockholder approval, or the board's failing to diligently seek competing offers. Fear that such litigation is not driven by merits but rather by the quest for a quick settlement is fed by a study finding no correlation between the premium shareholders receive as a consequence of the merger and the likelihood of there being a fiduciary class action claim. *See* Charles R. Korsmo & Minor Myers, The Structure of Stockholder Litigation: When Do the Merits Matter?, 75 Ohio. St. L. Rev. 829 (2014). The supposition is that shareholders sue when they believe they are not receiving a fair price for their shares due to the board's misconduct; a merger that produces a handsome premium to would thus be less likely to prompt complaint.

Page 1022.[2] Add the following after Note 3:

4. *Should Creditors Have Standing?* Chancellor William Allen famously observed in *Credit Lyonnais Bank Nederland N.V. v. Pathe Comm. Corp.*, 1991 WL 277613 *226 (Del. Ch. 1991) that when a corporation was in the "zone of insolvency," creditors should enjoy standing to raise fiduciary duty claims, reasoning:

> [W]here a corporation is operating in the vicinity of insolvency, a board of directors is not merely the agent of the residual risk bearers, but owes its duty to the corporate enterprise . . . [T]he board . . . had an obligation to the community of interest that sustained the corporation, to exercise judgment in an informed, good faith effort to maximize the corporation's long-term wealth creating capacity.

The Delaware Supreme court in *North American Catholic Education Programming Fdn. v. Gheewalla*, 930 A.2d 92 (Del. 2007) rejected *Credit*

---

[1]   Page 768 at the end of Background Note in Concise edition.
[2]   Page 770 in Concise edition.

Lyonnais's reasoning; the court instead concluded that creditors do not need protections beyond those they can secure through carefully crafted lending covenants and the panoply of remedies they enjoy under various creditor rights laws at the state and federal level. Nonetheless, some modest protections for creditors do exist under state corporate law and are summarized in *Quadrant Structured Products Co., Ltd. v. Vertin*, 115 A.3d 535 (Del.Ch. 2015):

i)   Directors owe a fiduciary duty to creditors only once a corporation is actually insolvent;

ii)   Creditors may only bring a derivative claim to enforce the directors' fiduciary duties;

iii)   Directors do not owe any particular duties to creditors, as their duty runs to the corporation for the benefit of all of its residual claimants that include the creditors of the insolvent firm;

iv)   Directors acting within their business judgment, can "favor certain non-insider creditors over others of similar priority;"

v)   Directors' ownership of stock does not alone give rise to a conflict of interest; and

vi)   The theory of deepening insolvency (where directors are alleged to breach their fiduciary duty by continuing to operate the firm with the consequence of increasing the losses to creditors) is rejected.

6.   THE DEMAND REQUIREMENT

Page 1059.[3] Substitute the following for *Aronson v. Lewis*:

Del. County Employees Ret. Fund v. Sanchez

Supreme Court of Delaware, 2015.
124 A.3d 1017.

■ STRINE, CHIEF JUSTICE:

. . .

This case involves an appeal from a complicated transaction between a private company whose equity is wholly owned by the family of A.R. Sanchez, Jr., Sanchez Resources, LLC (hereinafter, the "Private Sanchez Company"), and a public company in which the Sanchez family constitutes the largest stockholder bloc with some 16% of the shares and that is dependent on the Private Sanchez Company for all of its management services, Sanchez Energy Corporation (the "Sanchez Public Company"). The transaction at issue required the Sanchez Public Company to pay $78 million to: i) help the Private Sanchez Company buy out the interests of a private equity investor; ii) acquire an interest in certain properties with energy-producing potential from the Private

---

[3]   Page 801 of Concise edition.

Sanchez Company; iii) facilitate the joint production of 80,000 acres of property between the Sanchez Private and Public Companies; and iv) fund a cash payment of $14.4 million to the Private Sanchez Company. In this derivative action, the plaintiffs allege that this transaction involved a gross overpayment by the Sanchez Public Company, which unfairly benefited the Private Sanchez Company by allowing it to use the Sanchez Public Company's funds to buy out their private equity partner, obtain a large cash payment for itself, and obtain a contractual right to a lucrative royalty stream that was unduly favorable to the Private Sanchez Company and thus unfairly onerous to the Sanchez Public Company. . . .

The Court of Chancery dismissed the complaint, finding that the defendants were correct in their contention that the plaintiffs had not pled demand excusal under *Aronson [v. Lewis*, 473 A.2d 805 (Del. 1984)]. . . .

[I]n resolving this appeal, we focus on only one issue, which is outcome-determinative. The parties agree that two of the five directors on the Sanchez Public Company board were not disinterested in the transaction: A.R. Sanchez, Jr., the Public Company's Chairman [Chairman Sanchez]; and his son, Antonio R. Sanchez, III, the Sanchez Public Company's President and CEO. . . .

[handwritten margin note: 2|5 directors → ∅ disinterested]

The question for *Aronson* purposes was therefore whether the plaintiffs had pled particularized facts raising a pleading-stage doubt about the independence of one of the other Sanchez Public Company directors. If they had, the defendants and the Court of Chancery itself recognized that the plaintiffs would have pled grounds for demand excusal under *Aronson*.

III. ANALYSIS

To plead demand excusal under Rule 23.1, a plaintiff in a derivative action must plead particularized facts creating a "reasonable doubt" that either "(1) the directors are disinterested and independent or (2) the challenged transaction was otherwise the product 4 of a valid exercise of business judgment." Although there is a heightened burden under Rule 23.1 to plead particularized facts, when a motion to dismiss for failure to make a demand is made, all reasonable inferences from the pled facts must nonetheless be drawn in favor of the plaintiff in determining whether the plaintiff has met its burden under *Aronson*.

The closest question below centered on director Alan Jackson. The complaint bases its challenge to Jackson's independence on two related grounds. First, it pleads that "[Chairman] Sanchez and Jackson have been close friends for more than five decades." Consistent with this allegation, the complaint indicates that when Chairman Sanchez ran for Governor of Texas in 2012, Jackson donated $12,500 to his campaign.

Second, the complaint pleads facts supporting an inference that Jackson's personal wealth is largely attributable to business interests over which Chairman Sanchez has substantial influence. According to the complaint, Jackson's full-time job and primary source of income is as an executive at IBC Insurance Agency, Ltd. IBC Insurance provides insurance brokerage services to the Sanchez Public Company and other Sanchez affiliates. But even more importantly, IBC Insurance is a wholly owned subsidiary of International Bancshares Corporation ("IBC"), a company of which Chairman Sanchez is the largest stockholder and a director who IBC's board has determined is not independent under the NASDAQ Marketplace Rules. Not only does Jackson work full-time for IBC Insurance, so too does his brother. Both of them service the work that IBC Insurance does for the Sanchez Public and Private Companies. The complaint also alleges that the approximately $165,000 Jackson earned as a Sanchez Public Company director constituted "30–40% of Jackson's total income for 2012."

. . .

[E]mploying the *de novo* review that governs this appeal, we do not come to the same conclusion as the Court of Chancery. The reason for that is that the Court of Chancery's analysis seemed to consider the facts the plaintiffs pled about Jackson's personal friendship with Sanchez and the facts they pled regarding his business relationships as entirely separate issues. Having parsed them as categorically distinct, the Court of Chancery appears to have then concluded that neither category of facts on its own was enough to compromise Jackson's independence for purposes of demand excusal.

The problem with that approach is that our law requires that all the pled facts regarding a director's relationship to the interested party be considered in full context . . . . In that consideration . . . [the court is] bound to draw all inferences from those particularized facts in favor of the plaintiff, not the defendant, when dismissal of a derivative complaint is sought.

Here, the plaintiffs did not plead the kind of thin social-circle friendship, for want of a better way to put it, which was at issue in *Beam*. In that case, we held that allegations that directors "moved in the same social circles, attended the same weddings, developed business relationships before joining the board, and described each other as 'friends,' . . . are insufficient, without more, to rebut the presumption of independence." In saying that, we did not suggest that deeper human friendships could not exist that would have the effect of compromising a director's independence. When, as here, a plaintiff has pled that a director has been close friends with an interested party for a half century, the plaintiff has pled facts quite different from those at issue in *Beam*. Close friendships of that duration are likely considered precious by many people, and are rare. People drift apart for many reasons, and when a close relationship endures for that long, a pleading stage inference arises that it is important to the parties.

The plaintiffs did not rely simply on that proposition, however. They pled facts regarding the economic relations of Jackson and Chairman Sanchez that buttress their contention that they are confidantes and that there is a reasonable doubt that Jackson can act impartially in a matter of economic importance to Sanchez personally. It may be that it is entirely coincidental that Jackson's full-time job is as an executive at a subsidiary of a corporation over which Chairman Sanchez has substantial influence, as the largest stockholder, director, and the Chairman of an important source of brokerage work. It may be that it is also coincidental that Jackson's brother also works there. It may be coincidental that Jackson and his brother both work on insurance brokerage work for the Sanchez Public and Private Companies there. And it may be coincidental that Jackson finds himself a director of the Sanchez Public Company. But rather certainly, there arises a pleading stage inference that Jackson's economic positions derive in large measure from his 50-year close friendship with Chairman Sanchez, and that he is in these positions because Sanchez trusts, cares for, and respects him. . . . [W]here the question is whether the plaintiffs have met their pleading burden to plead facts suggesting that Jackson cannot act independently of Chairman Sanchez, these obvious inferences that arise from the pled facts require that the defendants' motion to dismiss be denied. In other words, using the precise parlance of *Aronson*, the plaintiffs pled particularized facts, that when considered in the plaintiff-friendly manner required, create a reasonable doubt about Jackson's independence.

. . .

Therefore, the judgment of the Court of Chancery of November 25, 2014 dismissing this case is reversed, and this case is remanded for further proceedings consistent with this opinion.

* * *

Sandys v. Pincus, 152 A.3d 124, 130–32 (Del. 2016), held that in considering whether the corporation should pursue claims of insider trading by the defendant a director who co-owned an airplane with the derivative suit defendant lacked independence. The court reasoned that co-ownership of an airplane, an unusual arrangement, "signaled an extremely close, personal bond . . . between their families." Two other directors were also deemed not to be independent to consider a demand because in public disclosures the company stated that its board did not consider either to qualify as an independent director under Nasdaq Listing Rules due to each being partners in the venture capital firm that controlled 9.2 percent of the company's stock. The court also observed the two directors had other relationships through other startups that "suggest . . . a mutually beneficial network of ongoing business relationships" that would be jeopardized were the two directors to support a corporation suing the defendants.

Page 1084.[4] Add the following after Note 5:

6. *The Demand Requirement and Preclusion in Multi-Forum Litigation.* Evidence of possible management misconduct frequently prompts litigation in multiple forums. Following a New York Times story detailing extensive bribery of Mexican officials and a coverup by senior executives of a Wal-Mart subsidiary, derivative suits were filed against certain Wal-Mart executives in the Delaware Chancery Court and the federal district court in Arkansas, Wal-Mart's headquarters. Different plaintiffs and law firms were involved in both the suits, but the complaints in both cases relied on facts set forth in the Times story. The Delaware proceeding was stayed after the Chancellor admonished its lawyers to "use the tools at hand," i.e., launch a books and records request, to sustain the otherwise unsupported allegations in the complaint, as otherwise the suit would not likely survive a motion to dismiss. Nearly three years passed due to the fierce resistance of Wal-Mart to the inspection request. During this period, the parallel suit in Arkansas was also stayed. However, the Eighth Circuit Court of Appeals ultimately vacated the stay and soon thereafter the Arkansas district court held that a pre-suit demand on the board of directors was necessary, had not been made, and dismissed the suit with prejudice. Wal-Mart thereupon moved for dismissal of the Delaware proceeding, arguing the Delaware plaintiff was collaterally estopped by the Arkansas holding from relitigating demand futility.

California State Teachers Ret. Sys. v. Alvarez, 179 A.3d 824 (Del. 2018), held that because the corporation is the real plaintiff in the derivative suit, privity thereby existed between the litigants in the two forums; the court further reasoned that Due Process is satisfied by the court scrutinizing the adequacy of representation in the Arkansas proceeding. Finding that counsel in that proceeding was adequate, the court held that Delaware plaintiff could not relitigate demand futility.

9. The Role of Corporate Counsel

Page 1107.[5] Add the following at the end of Note 1:

The Delaware Supreme Court in *Wal-Mart Stores, Inc. v. Ind. Elec. Workers Pensino Trust Fund IBEW,* 95 A.3d 1264 (Del. 2014), applied the *Garner* doctrine to permit a shareholder to review certain internal files that concerned what Wal-Mart directors knew regarding claims executives had paid bribes to facilitated business in Mexico. The shareholder document request was pursuant to shareholder inspection rights under Section 220 of the Delaware statute. Delaware previously had invoked *Garner* only in dicta.

---

[4]   Page 821 at the end of Note 3 of the Concise edition.

[5]   Page 840 of Concise edition.

10. SETTLEMENT OF DERIVATIVE ACTIONS

Page 1116.[6] Add the following at the end of the section:

Jill E. Fisch, Sean J. Griffith & Steven Davidoff Solomon, Confronting the Peppercorn Settlement in Merger Litigation: An Empirical Analysis and A Proposal for Reform, 93 Tex. L. Rev. 557 (2015), examine three types of relief flowing from challenged mergers: 1) amendment of the terms, 2) disclosure-only settlement, and 3) increase in merger consideration. They find amendment settlements and disclosure-only settlements do not have an impact on ultimate shareholder vote and there is only weak evidence that an increase in consideration impacts shareholder vote. They also tested other variables, finding that transaction value and the position of proxy advisors had significant effect. They reviewed transactions involving 453 firms in 2005–12 time period of which 319 experienced litigation and resulted in 191 involving the above-type of remedy. The study's authors recommend that state courts should, correlative with *Santa Fe v. Green*, 430 U.S. 462 (1977), *supra* Chapter 12, withdraw from disclosure-oriented challenges, remitting them to more experienced and institutionally equipped federal courts under the federal securities laws.

Disclosure-only settlements have caught the attention of the Delaware judiciary. Chancellor Bouchard provides a template for closer scrutiny of such settlements with *In re Trulia, Inc. Stockholder Litig.*, 129 A.3d 884 (Del. Ch. 2016):

> [D]isclosure settlements are likely to be met with continued disfavor in the future unless the supplemental disclosures address a plainly material misrepresentation or omission, and the subject matter of the proposed release is narrowly circumscribed to encompass nothing more than the disclosure claims and fiduciary duty claims concerning the sale, if the record shows that such claims have been investigated sufficiently. In using the term "plainly material," I mean that it should not be a close call that the supplemental information is material as that term is defined under Delaware law. Where the supplemental information is not material, it may be appropriate for the Court to appoint an *amicus curiae* to assess the Court in its evaluation of the alleged benefits of the supplemental disclosures given the challenges posed by the non-adversarial nature of the typical disclosure settlement hearing.

Id. at 898–99.

The complaint in *Trulia, Inc.* alleged the directors breached their fiduciary duties in approving a merger with a single bidder that allegedly failed to obtain the highest exchange ratio for the shareholders. Soon after the complaint was filed, opposing counsel reached an agreement in time for several supplemental disclosures to be added to the proxy statement circulated among the shareholders; the proposed settlement also provided the defendants would not oppose a fee request that did not exceed $375,000

---

[6]   Page 849 of Concise edition.

and the plaintiff class would broadly release any claims that could conceivably arise from the merger (except such claims that may exist under specified antitrust laws). The merger was ultimately approved by 79.52 percent of the shares entitled to vote (99.15 percent of the votes cast). Following the merger's completion, the parties sought approval of the settlement, which included any other claims that could be brought against the company's directors. Chancellor Bouchard closely examined each of the supplementary disclosures regarding distinct features of the valuation process used by the investment bank in its fairness opinion to the board. He found the supplementary disclosures were not meaningful in light of all the other information the company disclosed regarding the valuation process. He therefore rejected the settlement, thereby leaving the suit where it had started, a bald accusation of breach of fiduciary obligation.

Of additional interest in *Trulia, Inc.* is that the complaint did not allege that any disclosure violation on the part of the directors had occurred; the complaint essentially alleged the directors breached their *Revlon* duty, discussed in Chapter 15, in failing to aggressively shop the firm to obtain the best offer was received for the shareholders. Moreover, the settlement would release all (but certain antitrust) claims the class members may have against anyone arising from the merger. *Id.* at 890.

Trulia, Inc.'s likely reflects growing cynicism of deal-related litigation particularly the seemingly cosmetic recoveries their settlements produce. By way of background, consider that in 1999 and 2000 only 12 percent of deals produced litigation; in that era most of the deal litigation not only involved Delaware firms but also took place in Delaware. C.N.V. Krishnan, Ronald W. Masulis, Randall S. Thomas & Robert B. Thompson, Shareholder Litigation in Mergers and Acquisitions, 18 J. CORP. FIN. 1248, 1250–54 (2012). Suits in that era were consequential because firms that were sued experienced a statistically significant higher incidence of deals that did not close, and litigated deals that closed yielded their shareholders increased returns. Hence, the deal-focused suits in that former era could be seen, on the whole, as positive. Times have since changed. For example, Robert M. Daines & Olga Koumrian, Cornerstone Research, Shareholder Litigation Involving Mergers and Acquisitions: Review of 2012 M&A Litigation 1 (2013), reports that for deals valued over $100 million, 93 percent were challenged, with an average of 4.8 lawsuits filed per deal with a single deal often giving rise to litigation in more than one jurisdictions. Thus, unless we believe the mores within executive suites changed, and rapidly, the rapid increase in deal litigation more than likely points toward an abuse of process.

13. PRIVATE ORDERING AND SHAREHOLDER SUITS

Page 1137.[7] Add the following at the conclusion of the section:

Subsequent to *Boilermakers*, the Delaware Supreme Court, relying on the contract-orientation that was emphasized in *Boilermakers*, held that a non-stock Delaware corporation's board of directors could adopt

---

[7]   Page 858 of Concise edition.

and enforce a bylaw that shifted the defense's litigation costs to the plaintiff when the suit was not substantially successful. *ATP Tour, Inc. v. Deutscher Tennis Bund*, 91 A. 3d 554 (Del. 2014). It should be noted that Delaware non-stock corporations, although not having stockholders but members, are subject to the Delaware General Corporation Law.

To some extent, *Boilermakers and ATP Tour, Inc.* have now been overtaken by legislative developments. In 2015, the Delaware legislature amended the Delaware General Corporation Law to expressly authorize forum selection bylaws, Del. Gen. Corp. L. § 115, but that same legislature acted to prohibit fee shifting provisions, such as was involved in *ATP Tour, Inc.*, Del. Gen. Corp. L. § 102(f)(which prohibits the provision in the charter and by virtue of section 109(b) a fee shifting provision is also prohibited in the bylaws). Neither provision addresses another lurking development, bylaws calling for shareholder disputes to be arbitrated. S*ee* Ann Lipton, Manufactured Consent: The Problem of Arbitration Clauses in Corporate Charters and Bylaws, 104 Geo. L. J. 583 (2016). Commentators have also challenged the contractual basis for provisions affecting shareholder litigation via unilateral action by the board of directors. *See* James D. Cox, Corporate Law and the Limits of Private Ordering, 93 Wash. U. L. Rev. 257 (2015); Deborah A. DeMott, Forum Selection Bylaws Refracted Through the Agency Lens, 57 Ariz. L. Rev. 269 (2015); Lawrence A. Hamermesh, Consent in Corporate Law, 70 Bus. Law. 161 (2014). Query, could a board adopt a bylaw that requires a certain number of shares to be owned to initiate a derivative suit? How about a bylaw that conditioned the plaintiff initiating any kind of shareholder suit to post a bond to secure the defendant's litigation costs?

CHAPTER 15

CORPORATE COMBINATIONS, TENDER OFFERS AND DEFENDING CONTROL

1. CORPORATE COMBINATIONS

B. THE APPRAISAL REMEDY

Page 1148.[1] Insert the following at the conclusion of Note on the Appraisal Remedy:

Appraisal proceedings occur with sufficient frequency to be of concern to those involved in carrying out an acquisition. *See* Wei Jiang, Tao Li, Danqing Mei & Randall Thomas, Reforming the Delaware Appraisal Statute to Address Appraisal Arbitrage: Will It Be Successful, 59 J. L. & Econ. 697 (2016)(finding that of 1,566 Delaware-based corporations in 2000–2014 transactions for which the appraisal remedy was available, 225, or about 14 percent, were accompanied by formal appraisal proceeding and that the likelihood of a petition for appraisal is highly correlated with the relative premium offered by the deal over the pre-transaction market price). Another study found that the value of the holdings of the median appraisal petitioner in that study was $1.8 million, with a median percentage ownership of almost 1 percent of the affected company, Charles R. Korsmo & Minor Myers, The Structure of Stockholder Litigation: When Do the Merits Matter?, 75 Ohio St. L. J. 829 (2014). Jiang, et.al., while finding a similar median value for petitioners, report that about 32 percent of appraisal proceedings in their larger sample involved stakes below $1 million and constituted less than 1 percent of the company's stock. 59 J. L. & Econ. At 700. Korsmo & Myers found nearly three-fourths of the suits were settled; those that proceeded to trial yielded a 19.5% return over the merger consideration. *Id.* 878–882.

Beginning in 2007, the practice of "appraisal arbitrage" stimulated an increase in Delaware appraisal proceedings. Two legal developments likely contributed to this rise. *In re Transkaryotic Therapies, Inc.*, 2007 Del. Ch. LEXIS 57 (Del. Ch. May 2, 2007), held that a hedge fund could pursue appraisal for shares purchased after the transaction's record date without having to establish the shares had not earlier voted in favor of the acquisition (provided the shares held by a depository trust seeking appraisal must not exceed the total number of shares that did not vote in favor of the of the transaction). Also in 2007, the Delaware legislature confirmed that prejudgment interest on any sum recovered in appraisal would be the federal discount rate *plus 5 percent*. In an era of very low interest rates, the prejudgment rate was something of honey that attracted hedge fund bears.

---

[1] Page 868 in Concise edition.

To be noted here is that the Delaware statute did not then authorize, as does the Model Act, the company to reduce the amount of such pre-judgment interest by paying to the petitioner the amount offered pursuant to the merger's terms so that interest would be due only for any amount the stockholder gains above that amount via appraisal. *See* MBCA §§ 1324(a) & 1326(a).

In response to the above, in 2015 the Delaware appraisal provision was amended in several important ways. First, Section 262(h) was amended to mirror the Model Act's provision allowing the company to reduce the amount of the statutory pre-judgement interest by tendering some or all of the merger consideration to the appraisal petitioner. Second, Section 262(g) now requires a petitioner to hold a minimum of $1 million or 1 percent of the company's stock. An exception to this standing requirement exists for short-form mergers.

In an appraisal proceeding, how much weight, if any, should the court give to the price set in the merger negotiations if those negotiations are at arms-length? An earlier Delaware Supreme Court reasoned that according such deference would "inappropriately shift the responsibility to determine fair value from the court to the private parties." *Golden Telecom, Inc. v. Global GT, LP*, 11 A.3d 214, 218 (Del. 2010).

The Delaware Supreme Court in *Dell, Inc. v. Magnetar Global Event Driven Master Fund Ltd.*, 177 A.3d 1 (2017), pointedly criticized the Court of Chancery for failing to give any weight whatever to the "deal price" in determining value in an appraisal proceeding. In its post-trial decision, the Court of Chancery determined, based solely on its own discounted cash flow analysis, that the fair value of Dell Inc., at the time of the going-private transaction, was $17.62 per share, or approximately 28% above the $13.75 per share deal price. The Delaware Supreme Court observed: "[W]e agree with the Company's core premise that, on this particular record, the trial court erred in not assigning any mathematical weight to the deal price. In fact, the record as distilled by the trial court suggests that the deal price deserved heavy, if not dispositive weight." The Supreme Court further observed:

> The Court of Chancery identified three crucial problems with the pre-signing phase of the sale process that contributed to its decision to disregard the market-based indicators of value

> First, the primary bidders were all financial sponsors who used an LBO pricing model to determine their bid prices—meaning that the per-share deal price needed to be low enough to facilitate an IRR of approximately 20%. As the court saw it, the prospective PE buyers, the Buyout Group, Mr. Dell, and the Committee never focused on determining the intrinsic value of the Company as a going concern.

> Second, the trial court believed that Dell's investors were overwhelmingly focused on short-term profit, and that this "investor myopia" created a valuation gap that purportedly distorted the original merger consideration of $13.65. Thus, under the Court of Chancery's logic, the efficient market hypothesis—

which teaches that the price of a company's stock reflects all publicly available information as a consensus, per-share valuation—failed when it came to Dell, diminishing the probative value of the stock price. This phenomenon also allegedly depressed the deal price by anchoring deal negotiations at an improperly low starting point.

Third, the trial court concluded that there was no meaningful price competition during the pre-signing phase as, at any given time during the pre-signing phase, there were at most two private equity sponsors competing for the deal, creating little incentive to bid up the deal price. The trial court especially faulted the Committee for declining to reach out to potential strategic bidders, such as HP, during the pre-signing phase, leaving the financial sponsors who were engaged without the incentive "to push their prices upward to pre-empt potential interest from that direction." According to the trial court, large private equity buyers such as those engaged here are notoriously averse to topping each other, and without the specter of a strategic buyer, the Committee lacked "the most powerful tool that a seller can use to extract a portion of the bidder's anticipated surplus"—the "threat of an alternative deal."

Id. at 28–29.

The Supreme Court rejected each of the above three premises. First, with respect to the trial court's focus on the absence of strategic (as opposed to financial) bidders during the pre-signing market check, the Supreme Court observed it saw " 'no rational connection' between a buyer's status as a financial sponsor and the question of whether the deal price is a fair price." The Supreme Court emphasized that "Dell's sale process bore many . . . objective indicia of reliability" such as that Dell's investment bankers canvassed the interest of sixty-seven parties, including twenty possible strategic acquirers, during the forty-five day go-shop period. Second, the Supreme Court did not believe there was any basis to believe a gap existed between the firm's intrinsic value and its market price in light that Dell's stock was widely traded in a liquid and efficient market; it also believed the Company had been transparent about its long-term plans. Third, the trial court had credited expert testimony to the effect that management-led buyouts tend to suffer from structural problems, such as the "winner's curse" and the perceived value of management to the company, that undercut the reliability of the deal price as evidence of fair value. The concept of a "winner's curse" reflects the notion that "incumbent management has the best insight into the Company's value, or at least is perceived to have an informational advantage," so, if a financial buyer is willing to outspend management to win a deal, it must be overpaying because it must have overlooked some piece of information that dissuaded management from bidding as much. With regard specifically to the "winner's curse," the Supreme Court wrote: "If a deal price is at a level where the next upward move by a topping bidder has a material risk of being a self-destructive curse, that suggests the price is already at a level that is fair. The court reasoned that issue in an appraisal is not whether a negotiator has extracted the highest possible bid. Rather, the key inquiry is whether the dissenters got fair value and were not exploited." *Id.* at 63–64.

The Supreme Court concluded that the market-based indicators of value, including both stock price and deal price, had "substantial probative value." The Court also emphasized that Dell's sale process had "adopt[ed] many mechanisms designed to minimize conflict and ensure stockholders obtain the highest possible value," and noted that if a company's reward for adopting "best practices" in deal structuring is to be exposed to the risk of appraisal at a premium to deal price based on a discounted cash flow analysis, the incentives to adopt "best practices" would diminish.

The Delaware court has also strongly endorsed substantial weight being given to the firm's market price. *DFC Global Corp. v. Muirfield Value Partners, L.P.*, 172 A.3d 346, 372 (Del. 2017) ("When, as here, the company had no conflicts related to the transaction, a deep base of public shareholders, and highly active trading, the price at which its shares trade is informative of fair value, as that value reflects the judgments of many stockholders about the company's future prospects, based on public filings, industry information, and research conducted by equity analysts").

G. FREEZEOUTS

Page 1217.[2] Add the following at the end of Note on Delaware's Streamlined Back-End Merger Procedure:

In re Volcano Corp. Stockholder Litig., 143 A.3d 727 (Del. Ch. 2016), aff'd, 2017 Del. LEXIS 56 (Del., Feb. 9, 2017) addressed whether a merger carried out pursuant to 251(h) not only enjoys the presumption of the business judgment rule but also whether claims of wrongdoing on the part of the acquired company's board of directors are similarly protected. With the assistance of Goldman, Sachs, Volcano contacted five companies whether they had an interest in acquiring Volcano. No offer was forthcoming, but a sixth company, Phillips Holdings, made a non-binding indication of interest to acquire Volcano at $24 per share, subject to an eight-week exclusivity provision to permit Phillips to carryout due diligence. Volcano, while welcoming Phillips' interest (Volcano shares were then trading at $16.18 per share), nonetheless refused to grant Phillips any exclusive arrangement and communicated through Goldman, Sachs that the price would have to be above $24. In the ensuing weeks, weak performance by Volcano caused its stock to decline to $12.56 and Phillips reduced its offer to $17.25. This offer was rejected by Volcano. Five days later, Volcano presented a $16 per share offer and Volcano's board stated it would not consider an offer below $18. A week later, Volcano reported greater than expected earnings, Phillips raised its offer to $18, and the Volcano board approved a two-step transaction pursuant to Section 251(h), recommending that Volcano's shareholders tender their shares into the first-step tender offer. On February 17, 2015, the tender offer closed with 89.1 percent of Volcano's outstanding shares being tendered. That same day, the second-step merger was consummated.

---

[2]   Page 918 in Concise edition.

The quarrelsome Volcano stockholders' interest in challenging the transaction was piqued by several results flowing from the transaction. Before Volcano began to seek any strategic buyer it had engaged Goldman, Sachs as its underwriter for $460 million in convertible notes. Fearing that the notes' convertibility could harmfully dilute the ownership interest of its stockholders, Volcano and Goldman, Sachs entered into a series of derivative transactions that had the ultimate effect of raising substantially the price at which conversion of the notes would make financial sense. Not surprisingly, this had potential costs and benefits; Goldman, Sachs would benefit by a larger amount the earlier that any change in control transaction occurred. Thus, as a consequence of the merger with Phillips, Goldman, Sachs was entitled to receive $24.6 million payment from Volcano pursuant to the terms of the call/spread derivative transaction. Furthermore, Volcano's senior management received about $8.9 million as a result of the change of control accelerating options and restricted stock rights they had. And, the CEO obtained a range of severance benefits totaling $7.8 million. These items, however, were all sufficiently disclosed to Volcano's stockholders so the court believe full disclosure had occurred.

Central to the plaintiff's case was the belief that a merger carried out pursuant to Section 251(h) should not enjoy the business judgment rule presumption as does the typical straight merger such as that authorized by Section 251 because of differences between shareholders tendering their shares and shareholders voting.

> Two concerns have been raised [by the plaintiff] to support the argument that stockholder acceptance of a tender offer and a stockholder vote differ in a manner that should preclude the cleansing effect articulated by the Supreme Court in *Corwin* from applying to tender offers. Section 251(h) addresses each of those concerns. The first concern suggests that tender offers may differ from statutorily required stockholder votes based on "the lack of any explicit role in the [DGCL] for a target board of directors responding to a tender offer." A target board's role in negotiating a two-step merger subject to a first-step tender offer under Section 251(h), however, is substantially similar to its role in a merger subject to a stockholder vote under Section 251(c) of the DGCL. Section 251(h) requires that the merging corporations enter into a merger agreement that expressly "[p]ermits or requires such merger be effected under [Section 251(h)]." Because Section 251(h) requires a merger agreement, Sections 251(a) and (b) of the DGCL subject that agreement to the same obligations as a merger or consolidation consummated under any other section of the DGCL. For example, the target corporation's board must "adopt a resolution approving" that agreement "and declaring its advisability," and the merger agreement must provide "[t]he terms and conditions of the merger." The first-step tender offer also must be made "on the terms provided" in the negotiated merger agreement. And, in recommending that its stockholders tender their shares in connection with a Section 251(h) merger, the target

corporation's board has the same disclosure obligations as it would in any other communication with those stockholders. Taken together, therefore, Sections 251(a), (b), and (h) of the DGCL mandate that a target corporation's board negotiate, agree to, and declare the advisability of the terms of both the first-step tender offer and the second-step merger in a Section 251(h) merger, just as a target corporation's board must negotiate, agree to, and declare the advisability of a merger involving a stockholder vote under Section 251(c). The target board also is subject to the same common law fiduciary duties, regardless of the subsection under which the merger is consummated.

The second concern suggests that a first-step tender offer in a two-step merger arguably is more coercive than a stockholder vote in a one-step merger. Section 251(h), however, alleviates the coercion that stockholders might otherwise be subject to in a tender offer because (1) the first-step tender offer must be for all of the target company's outstanding stock, (2) the second-step merger must "be effected as soon as practicable following the consummation of the" first-step tender offer, (3) the consideration paid in the second-step merger must be of "the same amount and kind" as that paid in the first-step tender offer, and (4) appraisal rights are available in all Section 251(h) mergers, subject to the conditions and requirements of Section 262 of the DGCL. Thus, Section 251(h) appears to eliminate the policy bases on which a first-step tender offer in a two-step merger may be distinguished from a statutorily required stockholder vote, at least as it relates to the cleansing effect rendered therefrom. . . .

When a merger is consummated under Section 251(h), the first-step tender offer essentially replicates a statutorily required stockholder vote in favor of a merger in that both require approval—albeit pursuant to different corporate mechanisms—by stockholders representing at least a majority of a corporation's outstanding shares to effectuate the merger. A stockholder is no less exercising her "free and informed chance to decide on the economic merits of a transaction" simply by virtue of accepting a tender offer rather than casting a vote. And, judges are just as "poorly positioned to evaluate the wisdom of" stockholder-approved mergers under Section 251(h) as they are in the context of corporate transactions with statutorily required stockholder votes. . . .

I conclude that the acceptance of a first-step tender offer by fully informed, disinterested, uncoerced stockholders representing a majority of a corporation's outstanding shares in a two-step merger under Section 251(h) has the same cleansing effect . . . as a vote in favor of a merger by a fully informed, disinterested, uncoerced stockholder majority. . . .

143 A.3d at 741–47. The outcome in *Volcano Corp.* was greatly influenced by *Corwin v. KKR Fin. Holdings LLC*, 125 A.3d 304 (Del. 2015), that appears later in this chapter.

2. HOSTILE TAKEOVERS AND DEFENDING CONTROL

D. THE "REVLON MOMENT"

Page 1278.[3] Add the following at the end of Note on *Revlon* in Operation:

C&J Energy Servs. v. City of Miami Gen. Employees' & Sanitation Employees' Ret. Trust

Supreme Court of Delaware, 2014.
107 A.3d 1049.

■ STRINE, CHIEF JUSTICE:

I. INTRODUCTION

This is an expedited appeal from the Court of Chancery's imposition of an unusual preliminary injunction. City of Miami General Employees' and Sanitation Employees' Retirement Trust (the "plaintiffs") brought a class action on behalf of itself and other stockholders in C&J Energy Services, Inc. ("C&J") to enjoin a merger between C&J and a division of its competitor, Nabors Industries Ltd. ("Nabors"). The proposed transaction is itself unusual in that C&J, a U.S. corporation, will acquire a subsidiary of Nabors, which is domiciled in Bermuda, but Nabors will retain a majority of the equity in the surviving company. To obtain more favorable tax rates, the surviving entity, C&J Energy Services, Ltd. ("New C&J"), will be based in Bermuda, and thus subject to lower corporate tax rates than C&J currently pays.

To temper Nabors' majority voting control of the surviving company, C&J negotiated for certain protections, including a by-law guaranteeing that all stockholders would share *pro rata* in any future sale of New C&J, which can only be repealed by a unanimous stockholder vote. C&J also bargained for a "fiduciary out" if a superior proposal was to emerge during a lengthy passive market check, an unusual request for the buyer in a change of control transaction. And during that market check, a potential competing bidder faced only modest deal protection barriers.

Although the Court of Chancery found that the C&J board harbored no conflict of interest and was fully informed about its own company's value, the court determined there was a "plausible" violation of the board's *Revlon* duties because the board did not affirmatively shop the company either before or after signing. On that basis, the Court of Chancery enjoined the stockholder vote for 30 days, despite finding no reason to believe that C&J stockholders—who must vote to approve the transaction—would not have a fair opportunity to evaluate the deal for themselves on its economic merits.

---

[3]   Page 977 of Concise edition.

The Court of Chancery's order also required C&J to shop itself in violation of the merger agreement between C&J and Nabors, which prohibited C&J from soliciting other bids. . . .

We assume for the sake of analysis that *Revlon* was invoked by the pending transaction because Nabors will acquire a majority of New C&J's voting shares. But we nonetheless conclude that the Court of Chancery's injunction cannot stand. A preliminary injunction must be supported by a finding by the Court of Chancery that the plaintiffs have demonstrated a reasonable probability of success on the merits. The Court of Chancery made no such finding here, and the analysis that it conducted rested on the erroneous proposition that a company selling itself in a change of control transaction is required to shop itself to fulfill its duty to seek the highest immediate value. But *Revlon* and its progeny do not set out a specific route that a board must follow when fulfilling its fiduciary duties, and an independent board is entitled to use its business judgment to decide to enter into a strategic transaction that promises great benefit, even when it creates certain risks.[7] When a board exercises its judgment in good faith, tests the transaction through a viable passive market check, and gives its stockholders a fully informed, uncoerced opportunity to vote to accept the deal, we cannot conclude that the board likely violated its *Revlon* duties. It is too often forgotten that *Revlon*, and later cases like *QVC*,[8] primarily involved board resistance to a competing bid after the board had agreed to a change of control, which threatened to impede the emergence of another higher-priced deal. No hint of such a defensive, entrenching motive emerges from this record.

. . . .

III. ANALYSIS . . .

B. The Plaintiffs Have Not Demonstrated A Reasonable Probability Of Success On The Merits

1. The Court of Chancery's Ruling Rested on an Erroneous Understanding of What Revlon Requires of a Board of Directors

. . . *Revlon* involved a decision by a board of directors to chill the emergence of a higher offer from a bidder because the board's CEO disliked the new bidder, after the target board had agreed to sell the company for cash. . . .

Revlon does not require a board to set aside its own view of what is best for the corporation's stockholders and run an auction whenever the board approves a change of control transaction. As this Court has made clear, "there is no single blueprint that a board must follow to fulfill its

---

[7]   *See, e.g., Lyondell Chemical Co. v. Ryan*, 970 A.2d 235, 243 (Del. 2009); *Paramount Communications Inc. v. QVC Network Inc.*, 637 A.2d 34, 44 (Del. 1993) ("Delaware law recognizes that there is 'no single blueprint' that directors must follow."); *In Re Fort Howard Corp. S'holders Litig.*, 1988 Del. Ch. LEXIS 110, 1988 WL 83147 (Del. Ch. Aug. 8, 1988) (a pre-signing auction is not required where directors allowed for an effective post-signing market check).

[8]   *QVC*, 637 A.2d at 39.

duties," and a court applying *Revlon*'s enhanced scrutiny must decide "whether the directors made a *reasonable* decision, not a *perfect* decision."

In a series of decisions in the wake of *Revlon*, Chancellor Allen correctly read its holding as permitting a board to pursue the transaction it reasonably views as most valuable to stockholders, so long as the transaction is subject to an effective market check under circumstances in which any bidder interested in paying more has a reasonable opportunity to do so. Such a market check does not have to involve an active solicitation, so long as interested bidders have a fair opportunity to present a higher-value alternative, and the board has the flexibility to eschew the original transaction and accept the higher-value deal. The ability of the stockholders themselves to freely accept or reject the board's preferred course of action is also of great importance in this context.

Here, the Court of Chancery seems to have believed that *Revlon* required C&J's board to conduct a pre-signing active solicitation process in order to satisfy its contextual fiduciary duties. . . .

The Court of Chancery imposed a pre-signing solicitation requirement because of its perception that C&J's board did not have "an impeccable knowledge of the value of the company that it is selling." In so ruling, the Court of Chancery seemed to imply that *Revlon* required "impeccable knowledge," and that there was only one reasonable way to comply, *i.e.*, requiring a company to actively shop itself, which ignores the Court of Chancery's own well-reasoned precedent and that of this Court, including our recent decision in *Lyondell*. And the court's perception that the board was not adequately informed was in tension with its other findings, grounded in the record, that C&J's directors were well-informed as to Nabors CPS' value.

Nor does the record indicate that C&J's board was unaware of the implications of structuring the deal so that Nabors would have majority voting control over the surviving entity.[97] As the undisputed facts demonstrate, the C&J board was aware that Nabors would own a majority of the voting stock of New C&J, and indeed that such a shift in control was required to effect the tax-motivated re-domiciling that the board believed would be beneficial to C&J's stockholders. The board took steps to mitigate the effects of that change in control, including by providing that a two-thirds vote will be required to amend the corporate bye-laws, sell the company, or issue stock for a period of five years; and preventing Nabors from acquiring additional shares or selling its shares for the five year standstill period. Most important, the board negotiated for a by-law providing that all stockholders will receive *pro rata* consideration in any sale of the company or its assets, a by-law that cannot be repealed without unanimous stockholder approval.

Although we are reluctant in the context of this expedited appeal to conclude that these provisions were, in themselves, sufficient to take the

---

[97]   *See, e.g.*, App. to Opening Br. at 1750, 2377, 2383, 2539.

transaction out of the reach of *Revlon*, they do constitute important efforts by the C&J directors to protect their stockholders and to ensure that the transaction was favorable to them.

It is also important to note that there were no material barriers that would have prevented a rival bidder from making a superior offer. As discussed, the C&J board negotiated for a broad "fiduciary out" that enabled the board to terminate the transaction with Nabors if a more favorable deal emerged. . . . Therefore, if a competing bidder emerged, it faced only the barrier of a $65 million termination fee.[100] Further, the transaction was announced on July 25, and was not expected to be consummated until near the end of 2014, a period of time more than sufficient for a serious bidder to express interest and to formulate a binding offer for the C&J board to accept.

. . .

It is also contextually relevant that C&J's stockholders will have the chance to vote on whether to accept the benefits and risks that come with the transaction, or to reject the deal and have C&J continue to be run on a stand-alone basis.[104] Although the C&J board had to satisfy itself that the transaction was the best course of action for stockholders, the board could also take into account that its stockholders would have a fair chance to evaluate the board's decision for themselves. . . .

For these reasons, the Court of Chancery should not have issued any injunction at all.

Corwin v. KKR Fin. Holdings LLC

Delaware Supreme Court, 2015.
125 A.3d 304.

[The Delaware Supreme Court addressed the effect of shareholder approval on a claim that Financial Holdings' board breached its duty under *Revlon* in connection with KKR's acquisition of Financial Holdings. The acquisition was approved by both the independent directors of Financial Holding and the company's stockholders. Even though there were various contractual relations between KKR and Financial Holdings that limited Financial Holdings' discretion in some areas, the Chancellor concluded there was no evidence on which to conclude that KKR any power that would prevent Financial Holdings' board from exercising an independent judgment on the desirability of the merger or its terms. Hence both the Chancery Court and the Supreme Court concluded KKR was *not* a controlling stockholder so that the acquisition was not subject

---

[100] In the event that C&J stockholders reject the merger, C&J is required to pay Nabors $17 million in "fees and expenses," regardless of whether C&J engages in another transaction thereafter. Nabors Red Lion Limited Form S-4, as filed with the Securities and Exchange Commission on December 1, 2014, at 22, *available at* http://www.cjenergy.com/downloads/Nabors_Red_Lion_Limited_-_Form_S-4_-_Amendment_4.pdf.

[104] *See* note 88 *supra*.

to review pursuant to the entire fairness standard. The court therefore moved to consider whether *Revlon* provided relief to the plaintiffs.]

On appeal, the plaintiffs further contend that, even if the Chancellor was correct in determining that KKR was not a controlling stockholder, he was wrong to dismiss the complaint because they contend that if the entire fairness standard did not apply, *Revlon* did . . . .

The Chancellor agreed with that argument below, and adhered to precedent supporting the proposition that when a transaction not subject to the entire fairness standard is approved by a fully informed, uncoerced vote of the disinterested stockholders, the business judgment rule applies. Although the Chancellor took note of the possible conflict between his ruling and this Court's decision in *Gantler v. Stephens*, he reached the conclusion that *Gantler* did not alter the effect of legally required stockholder votes on the appropriate standard of review. Instead, the Chancellor read *Gantler* as a decision solely intended to clarify the meaning of the precise term "ratification." He had two primary reasons for so finding. First, he noted that any statement about the effect a statutorily required vote had on the appropriate standard of review would have been dictum because in *Gantler* the Court held that the disclosures regarding the vote in question—a vote on an amendment to the company's charter—were materially misleading.[18] Second, the Chancellor doubted that the Supreme Court would have "overrule[d] extensive Delaware precedent, including Justice Jacobs's own earlier decision in *Wheelabrator*, which involved a statutorily required stockholder vote to consummate a merger" without "expressly stat[ing] such an intention."

On appeal, the plaintiffs . . . argue that *Gantler* bound the Court of Chancery to give the informed stockholder vote no effect in determining the standard of review. They contend that the Chancellor's reading of *Gantler* as a decision focused on the precise term "ratification" and not a decision intended to overturn a deep strain of precedent it never bothered to cite, was incorrect. . . .

. . . No doubt *Gantler* can be read in more than one way, but we agree with the Chancellor's interpretation of that decision and do not accept the plaintiffs' contrary one. Had *Gantler* been intended to unsettle a long-standing body of case law, the decision would likely have said so. Moreover, as the Chancellor noted, the issue presented in this case was not even squarely before the Court in *Gantler* because it found the relevant proxy statement to be materially misleading. To erase any doubt on the part of practitioners, we embrace the Chancellor's well-reasoned decision and the precedent it cites to support an interpretation of *Gantler* as a narrow decision focused on defining a specific legal term,

---

[18] *Id.* ("The Supreme Court in *Gantler* did not expressly address the legal effect of a fully informed stockholder vote when the vote is statutorily required. Having determined that the proxy disclosures were materially misleading, the Supreme Court did not need [**12] to reach that question."); *Gantler*, 965 A.2d at 710.

"ratification," and not on the question of what standard of review applies if a transaction not subject to the entire fairness standard is approved by an informed, voluntary vote of disinterested stockholders. This view is consistent with well-reasoned Delaware precedent.

Furthermore, although the plaintiffs argue that adhering to the proposition that a fully informed, uncoerced stockholder vote invokes the business judgment rule would impair the operation of *Unocal* and *Revlon*, or expose stockholders to unfair action by directors without protection, the plaintiffs ignore several factors. First, *Unocal* and *Revlon* are primarily designed to give stockholders and the Court of Chancery the tool of injunctive relief to address important M & A decisions in real time, before closing. They were not tools designed with post-closing money damages claims in mind, the standards they articulate do not match the gross negligence standard for director due care liability under *Van Gorkom*, and with the prevalence of exculpatory charter provisions, due care liability is rarely even available.

Second and most important, the doctrine applies only to fully informed, uncoerced stockholder votes, and if troubling facts regarding director behavior were not disclosed that would have been material to a voting stockholder, then the business judgment rule is not invoked. Here, however, all of the objective facts regarding the board's interests, KKR's interests, and the negotiation process, were fully disclosed.

Finally, when a transaction is not subject to the entire fairness standard, the long-standing policy of our law has been to avoid the uncertainties and costs of judicial second-guessing when the disinterested stockholders have had the free and informed chance to decide on the economic merits of a transaction for themselves. There are sound reasons for this policy. When the real parties in interest—the disinterested equity owners—can easily protect themselves at the ballot box by simply voting no, the utility of a litigation-intrusive standard of review promises more costs to stockholders in the form of litigation rents and inhibitions on risk-taking than it promises in terms of benefits to them. The reason for that is tied to the core rationale of the business judgment rule, which is that judges are poorly positioned to evaluate the wisdom of business decisions and there is little utility to having them second-guess the determination of impartial decision-makers with more information (in the case of directors) or an actual economic stake in the outcome (in the case of informed, disinterested stockholders). In circumstances, therefore, where the stockholders have had the voluntary choice to accept or reject a transaction, the business judgment rule standard of review is the presumptively correct one and best facilitates wealth creation through the corporate form.

For these reasons, therefore, we affirm the Court of Chancery's judgment on the basis of its well-reasoned decision.

CHAPTER 17

THE PUBLIC DISTRIBUTION OF SECURITIES

4. THE REQUIREMENT OF REGISTRATION

B. THE INTRASTATE EXEMPTION

Page 1387.[1] Regulatory action update:

Exercising its broad rulemaking authority, in Securities Act Rel. No. 10238 (Oct. 26, 2016) the SEC amended existing Rule 147 and adopted new Rule 147A. Both safe harbor rules permit an issuer incorporated in a state other than its principal place of business to nonetheless be deemed a resident of the state of its principal place of business, which state can then be the focus of its intrastate offering. New Rule 147A is broader in its scope than Rule 147 because it requires only that purchasers be resident of the state in which the issuer is a resident. This feature of Rule 147A thus permits use of the Internet (a majority of the states have amended their Blue Sky Laws to authorize crowdfunding mechanisms) and other mass communication media to conduct intrastate offerings provide the issuer take reasonable steps to assure that each purchaser meets the local residency requirement. In contrast, offers conducted pursuant to Rule 147, and even Section 3(a)(11), are offer*ee* based so that each offeree must be a resident of the issuer's state. Another notable change introduced in 2016 is that the prescribed period during which resale restrictions must be in place was reduced to six months.

D. LIMITED OFFERINGS

Page 1396.[2] Update of regulatory action:

Securities Act Rel. No. 10238 (Oct. 26, 2016) introduced two significant changes to Regulation D. First, it raised the maximum offering amount for Rule 504 to $5 million. Second, in light of the liberalization of the Rule 504 exemption, the SEC repealed Rule 505.

Page 1400.[3] Update of regulatory action:

In Securities Act Release 9974 (Oct. 30, 2015), the SEC adopted final crowdfunding rules. The rules implement the provisions of the JOBS act summarized in the materials and, therefore, while consistent with the summary provided there are notably specific in their details as to the disclosure requirements to investors as well as the issuer's continuing

---

[1] Page 1037 in Concise edition.
[2] Page 1045 in Concise edition.
[3] Page 1049 of Concise edition.

disclosure requirements. The specific rules are set forth in 17 C.F.R. §§ 227.100 *et seq.*

E. REGULATION A

Page 1404.[4] Update of regulatory action:

In Securities Act Release 9741 (March 25, 2015), the SEC adopted new Regulation A providing for both Tier 1 and Tier 2 offerings consistent with the release set forth in the casebook. The final rules provide that Tier 2 offers are "covered securities" so that they are not subject to state blue sky review. Tier 1 offers, however, are subject to review. In advance of the SEC's action, the states revamped their coordinated review process so that review of Regulation A offerings is substantially shortened from what was the procedure earlier. The new Regulation A rules are set forth at 17 C.F.R. §§ 251–263.

F. TRANSACTIONS NOT INVOLVING AN ISSUER, UNDERWRITER, OR DEALER

Page 1417.[5] Insert the following before Note on the "4 1–1/2" Exemption:

(4) RESALES TO ACCREDITED INVESTORS

In 2015, Section 4(a)(7) was added to the Securities Act establishing a new resale transaction exemption. The exemption is available to any seller (except the issuer or its subsidiary) and is conditioned on each purchaser being accredited and there being no general solicitation or general advertisement in connection with the resale. Note the prohibition against general solicitation and advertisement parallels the same prohibition in Rule 502(c) of Regulation D.

The exemption provided in Section 4(a)(7) is purchaser, not offeree, based; therefore, a selling shareholder does not violate Section 5 if she mistakenly offers, but does not sell, the security to a person who is not accredited, so long as those that do purchase are each an accredited investor. When the issuer is not a reporting company certain basic information about the issuer as well as financial statements prepared according to generally accepted accounting principles (IFRs in the case of foreign issuers) must be made available to the purchaser. There is no information requirement if the issuer is a reporting company.

---

[4]   Page 1051 of Concise edition.
[5]   Page 1065 of Concise edition.